The Leadership Lexicon

A Handbook of Leadership Competencies with Skills and Development Actions

Rick Bellingham, Ed.D
William O'Brien, Ph.D.

HRD Press • Amherst • Massachusetts

Published by: HRD Press, Inc.
                22 Amherst Road
                Amherst, MA 01002
                (800) 822-2801 (U.S. and Canada)
                (413) 253-3488
                (413) 253-3490 (Fax)
                http://www.hrdpress.com

ISBN: 0-87425-855-3

Cover design by Eileen Klockars
Production services by Anctil Virtual Office
Editorial services by Suzanne Bay

Table of Contents

Acknowledgments

This book is a culmination of 25 years of work with leaders in over 200 organizations. We would like to acknowledge the contributions all of those leaders made to this book. It was their behaviors, after all, that gave us rich insights not only into the gap between theory and practice but also into the power of being able to combine all the essentials of leadership to improve organizational performance.

We have been students of leadership literature during our entire careers. We have read literally hundreds of books on leadership. While we found most of the books conceptual and hard to translate into real results, we did find useful jewels in most of the books. We therefore acknowledge the contributors to the literature on leadership.

This book emerged from work we were doing with the Merck Leadership Center. We were engaged to upgrade their leadership resource directory by identifying and describing observable behaviors that could be learned by Merck employees and be demonstrated through improved performance. Merck gave us permission to use the work we had done to create this book.

Our mentors over the years, Bob Carkhuff and Barry Cohen, clearly influenced our thinking about how this book should be organized. The construct of Identify—Build—Drive came from Barry. The idea that skills and behaviors need to support competencies and the notion that leadership can be de-mystified came from Bob. We acknowledge their profound contributions as thought leaders.

Several people contributed to this book. Rebecca Bellingham contributed significantly to the content supporting many of the competencies. Sarah Coogan helped with the content. Our family and friends have all weighed in on different aspects of the book. We acknowledge their loving contribution to our life and to our work.

Preface

The Leadership Architecture

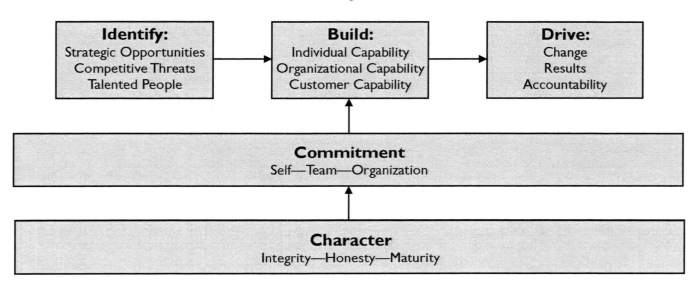

Leaders sometimes wonder why no one is following them. In most cases, the reason is because the leader does not possess all five essentials of leadership listed above. The first three essentials are the meta-competencies of leadership, and should be viewed as a process: Identify, Build, and Drive. Each of those three meta-competencies has a set of supporting competencies that this book describes in great detail. The three meta-competencies must be grounded by the two remaining essentials of leadership: character and commitment. Leaders must be honest and ethical at their core, or people won't follow. Leaders must also be committed to developing themselves and others. If people are not convinced of the leader's commitment to their growth, they will not help the leader grow—and they will not follow. The model above captures the architecture of great leadership—the five essentials that compel people to follow. The flowchart on the next page illustrates the context for leadership.

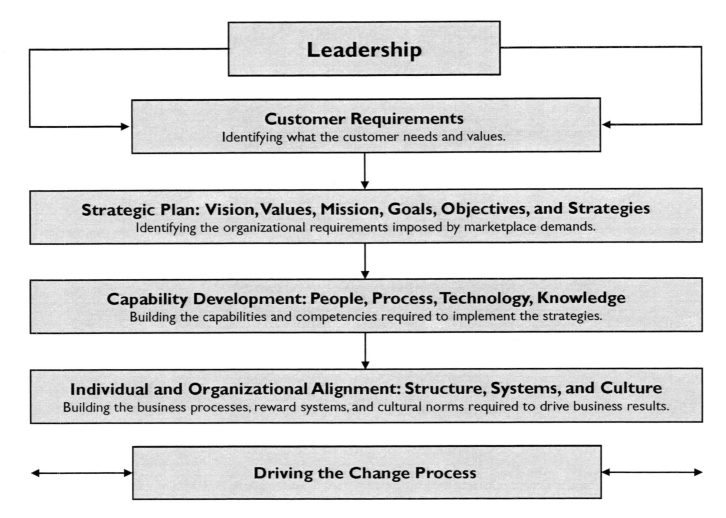

This chart illustrates the functions and flow of leadership. A great leader needs to identify customer requirements and strategic opportunities, build organizational capabilities and individual competencies, and align the infrastructure and culture behind the strategy. Simultaneously, a leader needs to drive the change process in a way that people will follow. This chart provides a high-level overview of great leadership.

The remainder of the book details the competencies, skills, and behaviors required to discharge these functions and optimize this flow. The Table of Contents lists the 100+ competencies required for extraordinary leadership. You will notice that the first 68 competencies support the meta-competencies of Identifying and Building.

Many leaders have the mistaken belief that driving for results is sufficient for effective leadership. Driving may be necessary, but it is clearly not sufficient. Driving for results, when combined with accurate identifying and genuine building, leads to successful implementation of the strategy. A "leader" who drives, but fails to identify or build, winds up with no followers. Leaders must possess all the essentials of leadership, and must pay attention to the flow and functions of leadership if they expect to have any followers.

Foreword

The reason why most people miss opportunity when it comes knocking is because it usually comes dressed in overalls, disguised as hard work.

—Thomas Edison

More than 20 years of research, consulting, and leading our own organizations have taught us one important principle above all else: all good ideas eventually degenerate into hard work. Edison had it right when he defined success as 99 percent perspiration and 1 percent inspiration. What a valuable lesson, especially when we consider the field of leadership development.

This book is the culmination of our observations and experiences regarding leadership and the process of becoming a skillful leader. If you are engaged or thinking about becoming engaged in a self-development process in order to increase your leadership effectiveness, we recommend that you learn and use the skills outlined in this book. However, before diving into the myriad skills, it is important to understand leadership in its proper context. Here are some principles to guide you in your development.

I. Leadership is not about charisma.

In 1990, the predominant prescription for managing change was to master the *art* of leadership. In fact, one often-cited remedy required executives to adopt and model a particular leadership "*style*" by reading books about barnstorming barbarians, Asian ancients, or modern-day moguls. But by the end of the decade, leadership as a personality trait that could help an individual manage complex change processes began to lose its luster.

The findings of a study by the World Economic Forum/Booze-Allen and the Hamilton Strategic Leadership Project (January 31, 2000) challenges the view still held by some investors, academics, and journalists that charismatic CEOs are the bedrock of successful enterprise leadership. The real challenge for senior management is to create an environment where desired behavior and results emerge naturally. Both studies suggest that it is not leadership style, but rather the creation of a collaborative culture that is the enduring legacy of successful change leaders.

2. Leadership requires skills.

Leadership development is best illustrated in the old joke about the man who is about to undergo elbow surgery. "The operation will be easy," the doctor says. "You'll be playing golf in two weeks." "That's just great," says the patient. "I've never played golf before." Golf is an appropriate metaphor for leadership development, and in fact, much has already been written on the "Zen" of golf, the "Tao" of golf, the "art" of golf, and the "chi" of golf. So what's our secret regarding the single biggest differentiator in golf? The answer is golf *skills*. How do people who swing golf clubs become good golfers? They take lessons. Here's another interesting statistic: Which professionals spend the most, per capita, on golf lessons? Did you guess CEOs? How about marketing VPs or sales executives? The answer is *professional golfers!*

It is also important to understand that skill development is different from knowledge development. Knowledge gives us an understanding of the behavior. Skills give us the capability to perform new behaviors. We get a perfect illustration of the difference between awareness and ability when we consider Olympic diving. After each dive, "experts" rate it with a degree of discrimination that requires an expert's knowledge and understanding of the sport. We don't however, see the experts don bathing suits and take the plunge. They do not possess expert performance ability, even if they have expertise. Indeed, they may have had such abilities in the past, but their performance has attenuated.

This brings us another important principle:

3. Skills, once learned, require constant development and feedback.

Why do golf pros spend so much time on lessons? After all, they have already "made it." As any golfer on tour will tell you, he or she is only as good as the *next* game. As an effective executive, manager, or individual contributor, you already understand that your future success has more to do with your current performance than your last big win. Leadership skills require continuous learning and feedback in order for you to improve your effectiveness and gain the maximum impact from what you've learned. This book is designed to introduce you to new skills, refresh your memory about skills you may already have learned, and hone or improve the skills you already possess. This book serves as your most important source for learning and strengthening the skills associated with leadership.

Continuous improvement requires feedback. Another reason why experts in all fields continue to receive coaching and mentoring is because of the feedback they receive on their performance. Receiving accurate feedback will determine the rate and efficiency of your leadership development. Relying on yourself for feedback is insufficient. The best sources of feedback are the individuals you coach and the individuals who coach you. Former New York City mayor Ed Koch, himself an author and lecturer on leadership, was famous for asking *"How am I doing?"* This constant refrain helped to brand him as the "people's mayor." He was a model for taking the risk of asking for genuine feedback from those whom he led.

4. Leadership is not a place in an organization.

Most of us think of leadership as a noun. For example, we often talk about "the leadership" in our company. However, leadership is also a verb. For us, leadership is not a hierarchical place on an organizational chart. Rather, leadership is the response that every employee makes to the challenge or opportunity at hand at any given moment. In every organization, "participants" do what's asked and "contributors" add value for themselves. However, "leaders" add value for themselves and others. We consider the three major activities for leaders at all levels to be (1) identifying new sources of gain, (2) building capabilities for yourself and others, and (3) driving goals to fruition.

Leaders follow a credo, whether they are individual contributors or they are high-ranking executives. First and foremost, they take all of their skill development to mastery. They soar past readiness, awareness, and acquisition and quickly move to real-life applications, feedback, and continuous learning. They not only view performance reviews as non-threatening, they consider them vital to their success! Leaders say what they will do and do what they say. Leaders manage expectations and then exceed them. Leaders prevent surprises. Leaders *win.*

5. Leaders stand out, for better or worse.

Dr. William Anthony, a leader in the transformation of policy and clinical practice in the mental health field, once described leadership as follows: "When the battle begins and the shots ring out, everyone is targeting the leader." Leaders often create the conditions for change. As a result, others are asked to do things differently. Leaders create new success criteria and change the rules of the game. By definition, then, leaders are often viewed as threats to the status quo and are often confronted by opposing forces. Anyone who tells you that he or she enjoyed the entire leadership experience has probably never experienced it in the first place.

Here's a description circa 1790 of Alexander Hamilton, co-author of The Federalist Papers, Constitutional visionary, and the single most important influence on shaping both the U.S. treasury and the federal government: "The bastard brat of a Scotch peddler, a Creole bastard who could scarcely acquire the opinions, feelings, or principles of the American People." We should also include this summary comment from Benjamin Franklin regarding John Adams: ". . . absolutely out of his senses." Throughout his entire term as our first president, General George Washington, founder of our country, was suspected by more than a third of the new nation's citizens of creating a glorious scheme to reunite America with England and be elevated to king.

These kinds of comments published in many newspapers throughout the colonies must have been discouraging and perhaps painful for these three men whom history correctly considers heroes and founding fathers. These examples illustrate that leaders often must be thick-skinned and very patient, and must be prepared to expect resistance, mistrust, misperceptions, and harsh criticism. Steve Ballmer, CEO of Microsoft, often tells the story of his mother asking him at an early stage in Microsoft's development why anyone would want to use a personal computer.

This is a book that offers each reader the opportunity to look deeply into the skills and behaviors that are associated with leadership. This is not a book designed to inspire you to lead; we assume that you are already motivated. Instead, this book identifies and describes the critical dimensions and core leadership skills that will improve your ability to make an impact.

What leaders require of those who follow is found in Edison's wise counsel: hard work. The content described in the following pages is indeed hard work. Take the time and discipline yourself to acquire and apply these skills. As professionals who have spent a great deal of time in New York City, we are reminded of the old adage about the tourist who asks, "How do you get to Carnegie Hall?" Practice, practice, practice.

Introduction

This book serves as a handy resource for practically any leadership challenge you will face. In a world in which on-the-job learning is all we have time for and/or all we can afford, this handbook provides down-to-earth suggestions for dealing with a wide range of leadership issues.

Effective leaders are able to identify opportunities and threats, develop the programs and teams required to meet those challenges, and drive for results. Those are the meta-competencies of leadership:

- Identify
- Build
- Drive

Few leaders are able to do what is involved in all three meta-competencies well. Most leaders are proficient in at least one competency, many leaders possess two of the three competencies, but very few have all three. This book peels the onion on those meta-competencies. In this book, we have identified over 100 competencies that support these three meta-competencies. For each competency, we have identified 5–10 skills required for proficiency in that competency. For each skill, we have provided 3–5 development suggestions that will improve your ability to lead. Thus, this book contains more than 500 leadership skills and more than 1,500 actionable suggestions. Yes, leadership is a daunting challenge. In this handbook, we offer concrete behaviors for enhancing your leadership skills.

In our 25-year experience with over 200 companies across the globe, we have concluded that the most effective leaders are DARING.

- **D**ecisive
- **A**ccurate
- **R**eflective
- **I**nnovative
- **N**etworked
- **G**rowing

We have been consultants to leaders in Fortune 50 companies as well as "mom and pop" operations, we have also concluded that the most DIRE results occur with leaders who have these characteristics:

- **D**ecisive
- **I**naccurate
- **R**esolute
- **E**vasive

In a complex world, it is much better to have a leader who tends to be indecisive until he or she has gathered sufficient information than to have a leader who is decisive but wrong. That problem is compounded when the leader is also resolute, because she or he refuses to change direction in response to changing conditions. The absolute worst leader is one who is decisive, inaccurate, resolute, *and* evasive. Evasive suggests that there is a lack of ownership in the problem and an unwillingness to confront the truth. You may want to use these criteria to evaluate political leaders around the world over the past 100 years. You will find that the most-positive results came from DARING leaders, and the most DIRE results came from hubristic leaders who made quick (but wrong) decisions and then failed to own responsibility for the outcome.

As you read this book, you will find some overlap in the behaviors supporting each competency. Since this book is designed to be a reference guide, we decided it would be better to have some redundancy than to leave out behaviors or skills that were particularly relevant to a respective competency. While we invite you to read the book from start to finish, you may find it more helpful to refer to the book as challenges arise in your organization. Based on our review of the literature and our extensive experience in the trenches with leaders in every type of organization, we feel confident that we have covered the full range of competencies required for effective leadership. We hope you find this book useful.

Chapter 1: Identifying
The First Meta-Competency

Introduction

Effective leaders are able to identify the right strategy, structure, people, processes, technology, and cultural requirements for meeting marketplace and customer requirements. This ability is not only based on experience and intuitive gifts, it also requires rigorous analysis of the conditions and standards operating in the marketplace. Great leaders are gifted in their ability to see possibilities *and* to be brutally honest about the reality of the situation. Seeing possibilities against the backdrop of realities is one of the most glaring attributes of effective leaders.

This chapter is divided into four sections:

    Section 1 Analyzing the Conditions and Possibilities
    Section 2 Honing Generic Skills and Establishing the Right Mind-Set
    Section 3 Developing the Plan and Priorities
    Section 4 Making the Hard Decisions

Doing the analysis means studying economic conditions, market opportunities, competitive threats, and organizational infrastructure and capabilities. These competencies characterize a leader who does his or her homework and who insists upon adequate decision support information.

Honing generic skills and establishing the right mind-set entails creating the conditions in which strategic thinking can occur. These competencies characterize a leader who understands that leadership requires more than "faking it." Leaders with these competencies are able to create an environment in which innovative thinking thrives.

Developing the plan and priorities takes into account all the analysis and leverages the environment to create a dynamic planning process that leads to great results. These competencies characterize a leader who takes a very systematic approach to planning and applies tremendous discipline to methodology. An effective leader ensures that an organization has a well-defined and articulated vision, mission, values, goals, objectives, strategies, and plans.

Making hard decisions means using the hard work and creative thought that emerged from the previous competencies to establish the right structure, to select the right people, and to develop the right processes for moving forward.

All of these competencies fall under the umbrella of identifying. Each of the competencies listed in this chapter will have supporting skills and behavioral suggestions you can use to enhance your leadership effectiveness.

Section 1—Analyzing the Conditions and Possibilities

Leadership Competency 1	Identifying Business Trends and Possibilities
Leadership Competency 2	Identifying Economic Factors and Possibilities
Leadership Competency 3	Identifying Financial Factors
Leadership Competency 4	Identifying Revenue Possibilities (Forecasting)
Leadership Competency 5	Identifying Global Business Possibilities
Leadership Competency 6	Identifying Organizational Factors

Leadership Competency 1: Identifying Business Trends and Possibilities

Skill: *Identify the impact of businesses going virtual.*

Actions:
- Explore ways to reach virtual businesses and teams.
- Understand the social networks that influence decision making.
- Seek out new ways to relate to virtual businesses that can help you run lean and that take little time.

Skill: *Understand the impact of technology on business.*

Actions:
- Explore ways that technology will impact your business and the business of your customers.
- Look for the opportunities and challenges of falling software and hardware prices.
- Keep abreast of the next "new thing" and how it could affect you.
- Subscribe to industry journals, join business groups to network and see what's going on, and watch the stock market.

Skill: *Understand the impact of the freelance economy.*

Actions:
- Understand how self-employment, contracting, and consulting have changed the nature of work.
- Explore ways to become leaner through the use of consultants and independent contractors.
- Look for the opportunities and threats that the freelance economy poses for you.

Skill: *Understand how business ecosystems proliferate.*

Actions:
- Understand how outsourcing has become the norm for many businesses.
- Look for more technology sharing within the ecosystems.
- Explore ways to leverage the ecosystem to find faster ways to initiate new ideas and processes.

(continued)

Leadership Competency 1:
Identifying Business Trends and Possibilities *(concluded)*

Skill: *Understand how globalization impacts business.*

Actions:
- Take advantage of instant communication world-wide.
- Explore how the proliferation of cheap communication technology has changed the shape of the global market.
- Expect a huge increase in translation services, import/export specialization, and other services across borders.
- Find partners who will enable you to expand your business globally.
- Read the latest books on global trends.

Leadership Competency 2:
Identifying Economic Factors and Possibilities

Skill: *Identify supply-side factors.*

Actions:
- Study the markets for your products, services, and solutions.
- Identify competitive products and determine if the market is saturated.
- Position your products on the life-cycle management curve as innovative, commercial, or commoditized. If your products are commoditized, then the supply exceeds the demand and you will need to compete through price.
- Ask yourself, "How would I position my products, services, and solutions on the product life-cycle management curve?"

Skill: *Identify demand-side factors.*

Actions:
- Study the demand for your products, services, and solutions.
- If you are introducing a new product to the market, you will need to create demand.
- Work closely with your marketing department to generate more demand for your products.

Skill: *Identify currency factors.*

Actions:
- Study how currencies vary throughout the world.
- Before you invest in an international market, understand the volatility of currencies.
- Work closely with your finance department to forecast how changes in currency may affect profitability.

Skill: *Identify balance-of-trade factors.*

Actions:
- Study international trade in order to understand the difference between imports and exports of countries in which you do business.
- Subscribe to *The Economist* or the *Financial Times* to learn more about trade agreements and import/export tariffs.

Skill: *Identify factors related to international markets.*

Actions:
- Search the Internet for international markets and go to links with market indexes for North America, Africa/Middle East, Asia/Pacific Rim, Europe, and South America.
- Look for risks, trends, and events in various countries that could affect revenues and expenses.

Skill: *Identify economic indicators and exposures.*

Actions:
- Study trends in interest rates, unemployment rates, the consumer price index, and housing.
- Join a group of colleagues who are discussing how changes in economic indicators could affect the business.

Leadership Competency 3:
Identifying Financial Factors

Skill: *Interpret financial results.*

Actions:
- Review revenue and expense reports.
- Analyze how the balance sheet has changed.
- Identify gaps between budgets and actual, and inquire about root causes for the variance.
- Identify strengths and weaknesses in your financial health.
- Ask yourself, "Are the cash-flow projections adequate to fund operating expenses?"

Skill: *Establish the break-even point.*

Actions:
- Identify the point at which revenues and expenses intersect.
- Understand what is required of sales to cover operating expenses.
- Compute cost of goods sold.

Skill: *Prepare and manage a cash-flow forecast.*

Actions:
- Create a chart that shows projected income and expenses on a monthly basis.
- Compute cash on hand and project incoming cash on a monthly basis.
- Analyze accounts payable and project the outflow of cash on a monthly basis.
- Ask yourself, "Do we anticipate having sufficient cash to handle our operating expenses?" Develop a plan to address projected deficits and surpluses.

Skill: *Prepare and manage operational budgets.*

Actions:
- Write down all sources of revenue for an entire year on a month-to-month basis.
- Write down all anticipated expenses for an entire year on a month-to-month basis.
- Prepare and analyze line item variations monthly.
- Take corrective action as needed.

Skill: *Measure financial performance.*

Actions:
- Analyze revenues and expenses.
- Compute return on equity, return on investment, and net income.
- Analyze revenue per employee, and compare that figure to industry norms.
- Analyze sales productivity and compare it to industry norms.
- Subscribe to *Financial Times* or take a course in finance.

Leadership Competency 4:
Identifying Revenue Possibilities (Forecasting)

Skill: *Assess economic conditions.*

Actions:
- Study the growth/decline in gross national product in all of the countries in which you are doing business.
- Study multiple sources of input to get a sense of projections and trends.
- Join a group of colleagues to discuss macro economic trends and how they might affect the business.

Skill: *Assess market conditions.*

Actions:
- Study the verticals and horizontals in which you do business.
- Analyze changes in competition and changes in customer buying patterns.
- Ask yourself, "What are the key business drivers for making purchasing decisions in my market?"

Skill: *Assess product demand.*

Actions:
- Study trend lines for your products, services, and solutions.
- Identify which products are growing and which seem to be declining.
- Read analyst reports on your products and on competitive products.

Skill: *Assess seasonality.*

Actions:
- Analyze sales per quarter over the past three years.
- Identify any seasonal factors that may be causing disruptions in revenue.
- Ask yourself, "What do I need to do to flatten the hockey stick or adjust to seasonal variations?"

Skill: *Assess competition.*

Actions:
- Keep abreast of what the competition is doing.
- Stay current on changes in prices, products, promotions, and places where your competitors are doing business.
- Identify your competitive differentiation in all products, markets, distribution channels, and geographies.

Skill: *Predict sales.*

Actions:
- Based on your assessment and analysis of the economy, the market conditions, product demand, and competitive threats, forecast sales on a monthly basis.
- Ask yourself, "On what assumptions am I basing these predictions?"
- Invite your colleagues to challenge your assumptions.

Leadership Competency 5:
Identifying Global Business Possibilities

Skill:	*Understand global markets.*
Actions:	• Subscribe to journals that cover international markets. • Use the Internet to study economic indexes in countries in which you do business.

Skill:	*Understand the impact of political changes.*
Actions:	• Keep abreast of global politics. • Subscribe to *The New York Times* and read the international news section. • Join a discussion group and engage in dialogue about the impact of political changes on the business.

Skill:	*Understand outsourcing possibilities.*
Actions:	• Stay current with outsourcing trends. • Analyze your function to determine if there are any aspects you could consider outsourcing. • Form a task force to explore the pros and cons of outsourcing particular functions in your organization.

Skill:	*Understand global competition.*
Actions:	• Identify your biggest competitors in each geographic region. • Study how they differentiate themselves from you. • Ask yourself, "Does our value proposition clearly differentiate us from our competition?"

Skill:	*Understand different cultures and ways of doing business.*
Actions:	• Participate in meetings in which the subject is doing business in another country. • Identify the cultural threats and opportunities for your business. • Ask yourself, "Are we taking into account the cultural differences in the countries in which we are doing business?"

Skill:	*Understand the global economy.*
Actions:	• Keep track of economic indicators in Asia, Africa, the Middle East, Europe, and Latin America. • Subscribe to journals that focus on global economic issues.

Leadership Competency 6:
Identifying Organizational Factors

Skill: *Identify how people have changed.*

Actions:
- Reflect on the staffing changes that have occurred and are likely to occur.
- Identify the ways in which those staffing changes could affect you.
- Ask yourself, "With whom do I need to build a positive relationship in this new organization?"

Skill: *Identify how processes have changed.*

Actions:
- Identify how business processes have changed.
- Identify the core processes in your organization and in the organizations with whom you have interdependencies.
- Ask for process maps in those organizations and inquire how they have changed.

Skill: *Identify how technology has changed.*

Actions:
- Keep abreast of changes in technology.
- Seek to understand how new technologies impact you and the business.
- If possible, take courses in the technologies that are relevant to you.
- Be aware of new technologies, keep acquiring new technology skills, and practice using new technology to improve your marketability and your results.

Skill: *Identify how culture has changed.*

Actions:
- Know the core values of your organization.
- Post a copy of the operating principles or norms (if they exist) in your office area.
- Identify which values are most important to you.
- Ask yourself, "Which of these values are the strongest, and which are getting better or getting worse?"
- Get a sense of how well the culture is aligned with the strategy at different points in time.

Skill: *Identify how strategy has changed.*

Actions:
- Keep informed of changes in company, organizational, or departmental strategy.
- Read annual reports and attend "town meetings."
- Ask your boss how the strategy is changing.

(continued)

Leadership Competency 6:
Identifying Organizational Factors *(concluded)*

Skill: *Identify how knowledge has changed.*

Actions:
- Stay current on changes in the knowledge base.
- Keep informed of new developments or databases.
- Find out if there are shared workspaces where you can access information.
- Identify the best sources of information in your organization, and stay in contact with them.
- Be a part of the social network.

Section 2—Honing Generic Skills and Establishing the Right Mind-Set

Leadership Competency 7	Creativity
Leadership Competency 8	Innovation
Leadership Competency 9	Strategic Thinking
Leadership Competency 10	Mind Mapping
Leadership Competency 11	Organizational Learning
Leadership Competency 12	Continuous Learning

Leadership Competency 7: Creativity

Skill: *Reward autonomous functioning, initiative, and creativity.*

Action:
- Openly recognize and reward autonomous functioning, initiative, and creativity in team members.

Skill: *Suspend your critical judgment during the creative process.*

Action:
- In the creativity phase, suspend your critical judgment—that part of you that says, "It won't work." Instead, think in positive terms: "It might work, because . . ."

Skill: *Try drawing problems instead of writing them down.*

Action:
- To further stimulate your creativity, try drawing a diagram of the problem instead of writing it down in words.

Skill: *Be open to multiple perspectives.*

Actions:
- Involve people of diverse backgrounds, beliefs, ages, life experience, etc., in discussion and problem solving.
- Listen to people with different ideas than your own, and be open to learning from their perspective.
- Expose yourself to new ways of thinking, approaching, and doing things through interaction with different kinds of people, experiences, and ideas.

Skill: *Find hidden connections and possibilities.*

Actions:
- Don't judge an idea before exploring the possibilities it might have or the ways in which it might serve as a solution for other problems or issues.
- Allow enough time for you and others to make important and potentially generative associations with the idea at hand.
- Let yourself freely associate, in order to see where your mind or thoughts go. Does this idea trigger thoughts or bring to mind something exciting, useful, or fresh?

(continued)

Leadership Competency 7:
Creativity *(concluded)*

Skill: *Identify people who are open to new possibilities.*

Actions:
- Believe that everyone has the power to be creative and innovative, and treat everyone, including yourself, as a generator of possibilities.
- Give yourself permission to imagine and dream up seemingly impossible, even absurd, scenarios, solutions, or ideas.
- Allow people time to think, reflect, and imagine in order to tap into their inner creativity and thoughtfulness.
- Forget the myth that only special people are creative.

Skill: *Assess your own level of creativity.*

Action:
- Ask yourself how open you are to new ideas. What kind of thinker are you? Are you realistic, analytical, idealistic, radical? What ways could you challenge yourself to think differently? When was the last time you challenged yourself to understand or look at something from a different perspective? Are you stuck in certain patterns of thinking or doing things? How could you push or stretch yourself in new ways in order to open yourself up to new ideas or solutions?

Skill: *Minimize the fear of taking risks.*

Actions:
- Recognize that creativity and taking risks go hand-in-hand.
- Be open about your own mistakes, and tolerate mistakes or failure in others when they have tried something new without success.
- Take time to reflect and learn from mistakes so that people see the value in taking risks and learning from them, instead of being afraid to try new things.

Skill: *Reward creativity and innovation.*

Actions:
- Find ways to reward employees who have generated creative solutions. Give them both tangible rewards (adequate workspace, budget, promotions, etc.) and intangible rewards (special attention, public credit for their ideas, challenging tasks).
- Praise people for thinking outside the box.

Skill: *Remove barriers to creativity.*

Actions:
- Take time to have fun and restore yourself so that creativity can spring up within you.
- Give yourself and others appropriate blocks of time for thinking, reflecting, meditating, making lists, brainstorming, free-associating, making leaps of the imagination.
- Allow this time to be "censor-free"—no evaluating, criticizing, or judging. Often the longer the list of ideas, the higher the quality of the final solution (the best ideas often appear at the end of the list).

Leadership Competency 8:
Innovation

Skill: *Use innovation techniques for problem solving.*

Action: • Learn more about such innovation techniques as brainstorming,
              storyboarding, and mind mapping, and apply them in your group
              for planning and problem solving.

Skill: *Encourage innovation in your department.*

Actions: • Set aside time at your regular staff meetings to discuss new, innovative ideas.
              • Create a climate in which people initially encourage, rather than criticize,
                new ideas; ask people to first discuss what they like and the possibilities
                associated with the idea, rather than focus on what they dislike or possible
                obstacles.
              • Foster the attitude that innovative thinking is part of everyone's job, regard-
                less of function or level of responsibility. Do this by openly acknowledging
                good ideas and thanking individuals who come up with them.

Skill: *Increase your mental flexibility.*

Actions: • Watch for snap reactions in yourself and when responding to others.
              • Instead of assuming that your first alternative or idea is the best one,
                write it down and consider other options.
              • Listen to and build on other people's opinions and ideas by adopting a
                "yes, and" instead of a "yes, but" attitude.
              • Ask yourself whether or not you are being too rigid or inflexible about
                certain ideas or approaches, and whether or not you are stuck on one
                answer, process, method, solution, etc.

Skill: *Stimulate creative ideas and experimentation in others.*

Actions: • Allow time for ideas to brew before asking for a solution that can
                be implemented.
              • Remember that creativity cannot always be produced on demand.
                Give people time to think and meditate on things.

Skill: *Challenge the way it has always been done.*

Actions: • Question status-quo assumptions and processes by challenging statements
                that close off alternatives ("It has to be done like this," "They'll never
                accept . . ., "We can't . . .").
              • Reward and acknowledge employees who are flexible and have "can-do"
                attitudes. Eliminate organizational barriers that keep people stuck in the
                status-quo, and find ways to remove barriers when possible.

(continued)

Leadership Competency 8:
Innovation *(concluded)*

Skill: *Champion new ideas and initiatives.*

Actions:
- Become a "change champion" by shifting your "If it's not broken, don't fix it" attitude to "If it isn't broken, look to see how it can be improved. Things can always be better."
- Create a clear, compelling vision for new processes or initiatives, the reasons for them, and the benefits to the business and those who will be impacted.
- Identify the people whose support you need in order to implement new ideas and initiatives and find ways to involve them.

Skill: *Support those who generate innovative ideas and processes.*

Actions:
- Protect "idea" people (who are sometimes viewed suspiciously) by making sure others understand the value of innovation and appreciate people who generate new ways of thinking and doing.
- Provide opportunities for innovators to network and learn what other innovators are doing (seminars, workshops, professional meetings, etc.).

Skill: *Approach problems with curiosity and open-mindedness.*

Actions:
- To get your creative juices flowing and reduce your self-criticism, practice coming up with what may at first seem like "way-out" ideas.
- Avoid prematurely censoring ideas, and don't be concerned about whether ideas are flowing in a logical sequence.
- Constantly expose yourself to new ideas and trends by reading newspapers, books, and journals and by talking to people from different backgrounds and generations so that you get fresh perspectives.

Leadership Competency 9: Strategic Thinking

Skill:	*Clearly communicate your organization's business plan.*
Action:	• Clearly communicate your organization's business plan so that your team can effectively build its own strategies.

Skill:	*Encourage the team to gather information and benchmark to make better decisions.*
Action:	• In preparation for making a major decision, encourage the team to gather information and/or benchmarking from at least three sources before making an "off-the-cuff" decision.

Skill:	*Evaluate the business and financial data you regularly receive.*
Actions:	• Evaluate all of the business and financial data you regularly receive (electronically or otherwise), and make it available to your team within the limits of confidentiality guidelines. • Ask team members what information they would like to have in order to do their jobs better. If it is not available, find out how to obtain it on a regular basis. • Make a habit of reading key business literature (e.g., *Business Week, Fortune, The Wall Street Journal,* etc.) to keep on top of business developments that might affect the company.

Skill:	*Learn from experts in another function.*
Actions:	• Invite an expert from another function or a visiting leader from an international group to talk to your team about the implications of new strategies and how they relate to your team. • Interview key stakeholders in different functions or at different levels to gain an understanding of their perspectives.

Skill:	*Review the organization chart.*
Actions:	• Review the organization chart to get a sense of how the business operates. • Participate on a task force outside your function to get a hands-on feel for how strategic thinking is promoted in other organizations.

Leadership Competency 10:
Mind Mapping

Skill:	*Strengthen your imagination.*
Actions:	• Free yourself to think speculatively. • Explore possibilities before judging them. • Look for non-routine or conventional solutions. • Take a course in creative thinking.

Skill:	*Unlock the potential of the brain.*
Actions:	• Harness the full range of brain skills: word, image, number, logic, rhythm, color, and spatial awareness. • Roam the expanses of your brain. • Apply mind mapping to every aspect of your life. • Read a book by Tony Buzan.

Skill:	*Overview a large subject area.*
Actions:	• Try to create the big picture and represent it graphically. • Establish routes to let you know where you are going.

Skill:	*Create a mind map.*
Actions:	• Start by writing down a central word. • Write 5–10 main ideas around the word. • Focus on a key idea and write down supporting ideas. • Use lines and arrows to see how the ideas connect. • Create a visual diagram of your thought process. • Look for connecting links.

Skill:	*Use software tools to strengthen your mind-mapping capabilities.*
Actions:	• Explore different visual mind-mapping software (e.g., Mind Manager, Visual Mind Graph, The Brain, Mind Genius). • Use these tools to "diagram" your creative ideas.

Skill:	*Make meetings productive.*
Actions:	• Start meetings on time. • State the purpose and agenda before the meeting, if possible. • Engage in problem-solving activities. • Use big whiteboards to frame problems and show the interrelationships among different solutions and issues.

Leadership Competency 11: Organizational Learning

Skill: *Identify the characteristics of a learning organization.*

Actions:
- Make sure that policies reflect the values of all members of the organization.
- Use information for understanding vs. punishment.
- Encourage people to speak freely and candidly with each other.
- Provide flexible working patterns, and allow people to make different contributions and draw different rewards.

Skill: *Develop the capabilities needed in order to drive a "learning" organization.*

Actions:
- Start with the goals of the business.
- Ask yourself:
  — What knowledge is needed, and where does it reside?
  — What do I need to do to improve collaboration between and among groups?
  — What processes do I need to build to improve learning and customer growth?
  — What technology do I need to support learning?

Skill: *Define the components of a learning organization.*

Actions:
- Make sure everyone is involved in the creation of a learning organization.
- Involve senior leadership, marketing, sales, finances, legal, IT, and operations.
- Strive for inclusiveness.

Skill: *Shape the culture to support a learning organization.*

Actions:
- Articulate the values and norms that support organizational learning.
- Ask yourself, "How well do we experiment, inquire, envision, collaborate, and strategize?"
- Conduct a learning culture audit once a year.

Skill: *Broaden your view of capital development.*

Actions:
- Think of capital development in more than financial terms.
- Ask yourself what you can do to develop information capital, human capital, organizational capital, customer capital, and community capital.

Leadership Competency 12:
Continuous Learning

Skill: *Take personal criticism without showing defensiveness.*

Actions: • Be more willing to take personal criticism without showing defensiveness.
          • Ask yourself how often you are saying "Yeah, but" or "But I" in response to personal criticism. One good way to make sure that you are not coming across defensively is to discipline yourself to re-state the criticism in your own words to make sure you understand exactly what the criticism is.

Skill: *Conduct a customer survey.*

Actions: • Conduct a customer survey to determine the products/services most needed by your customers.
          • Actively solicit information regarding how your activities and projects are impacting others (positively and negatively).

Skill: *Confront problems instead of avoiding them.*

Actions: • When you put off dealing with a problem situation, ask yourself why.
          • Learn to lean into your areas of discomfort in order to improve your skills and knowledge.
          • Ask for help from a respected colleague if you are finding it difficult to take the initiative required to reduce a deficit or learn a new skill.

Skill: *Sponsor a continuous learning initiative.*

Action: • Take responsibility for and develop the habits and practices for rapid and continuous learning initiatives through activities such as: self-study projects; development and tracking of personal learning goals; participation in and support for a team learning environment.

Skill: *Decide on a clear-cut, long-range goal for yourself.*

Action: • Then establish what you will need to do; what competencies, skills, and knowledge are required; and what attitudes you will need to have in order to achieve it.

Skill: *Develop a network of colleagues.*

Actions: • Develop a network of colleagues in areas that can help you with planning and organizing projects (i.e., finance, sourcing, etc.).
          • Select people you like who think interdependently and to whom you have convenient access.

(continued)

Leadership Competency 12:
Continuous Learning *(continued)*

Skill: *Develop a learning network.*

Action:
- Create a wide network of personal contacts through involvement in special study experiences (such as at top business/technical schools); initiatives to make and maintain contacts with professionals inside and outside the company (e.g., industry associations); and activities that produce a visible identity within the company for an area of personal expertise.

Skill: *Find something you can learn from each person with whom you work.*

Action:
- Ask yourself: What knowledge, skills, and attitude does this person possess that I can learn from?

Skill: *Find ways to leverage your strengths.*

Actions:
- First, identify five of your greatest strengths.
- Then explore ways you can apply those strengths to three specific problems or opportunities you are facing.

Skill: *Gain feedback from others by using a multi-rater assessment.*

Actions:
- Consider using a multi-rater or 360-degree feedback instrument to obtain comprehensive feedback on your skills from others.
- Learn to look at negative feedback and criticism as potentially useful information that you need to understand more fully.

Skill: *Keep track of lessons learned.*

Actions:
- Keep track of lessons learned, and refer to them periodically to reinforce your learning.
- Keep a "lessons learned" notebook on your desk.
- Learn for the sake of gaining wisdom, not just knowledge.

Skill: *Use root-cause analysis techniques.*

Actions:
- Learn root-cause analysis techniques (e.g., fishbone diagrams, "5 ways," etc.).
- For each problem, try to identify three, four, or five factors that account for 80 percent of the problem.

Skill: *Observe how you change and adapt because of what you have learned.*

Actions:
- Examine what you do with the lessons you learn from feedback and experience.
- Observe how you change and adapt, based on these lessons.
- Commit to being a lifelong learner.
- Approach every situation by asking yourself, "What can I learn?"

(continued)

Leadership Competency 12:
Continuous Learning *(concluded)*

Skill: *Put your development goals on your daily to-do list.*

Actions: • Review your calendar daily.
                • Identify at least one time in the day that you can practice a behavior or skill you are trying to learn or fine-tune.

Skill: *When you make a mistake, learn from it.*

Action: • For each project, ask yourself what worked, what didn't work, what would have needed to happen to improve performance, and how you can apply this learning to the next project.

Section 3—Developing the Plan and Priorities

Leadership Competency 13	Visioning and Positioning
Leadership Competency 14	Communicating the Vision
Leadership Competency 15	Strategic Planning
Leadership Competency 16	Setting Goals
Leadership Competency 17	Setting Objectives
Leadership Competency 18	Planning and Organizing
Leadership Competency 19	Resource Planning
Leadership Competency 20	Developing a Business Plan
Leadership Competency 21	Setting Priorities

Leadership Competency 13: Visioning and Positioning

Skill: *Lead a visioning workshop to align team goals with business goals.*

Actions:
- Develop scenarios for your team about what it will be doing five years from now.
- Generate specific communication plans for important activities that support the strategic vision.

Skill: *Play a role in turning around an image problem.*

Action:
- Play a significant role in a situation where the company's reputation is in jeopardy and where you can help assess the situation; raise the level of communication, trust, and teamwork; take quick, firm action; and help rebuild confidence within the team and with the customer.

Skill: *Create a shared vision.*

Actions:
- Capture the imagination of others by communicating a clear sense of the organization's purpose and mission.
- Set aside time for discussion, reflection, and clarification of the organization's vision and mission.
- Ask yourself and others if this vision matches the image you and they hold for the future.

Skill: *See problems and understand issues before others do.*

Actions:
- Try to identify problems, threats, and trends before they become crises.
- Stay alert to what is happening in your organization, other organizations, and the marketplace. Do you notice developments that could have an impact on your organization?
- Discuss your observations with colleagues, and tap the knowledge and expertise of people who are known for recognizing key trends.

(continued)

Leadership Competency 13:
Visioning and Positioning *(concluded)*

Skill: *Generate fresh perspectives and innovative ideas that might make a positive impact on your business and market positioning.*

Actions: • Challenge yourself to think outside of the box and shake up your thinking.
               • Ask yourself if there is a better idea out there that might prove more effective.
               • Seek out other people's perspectives, and be open to looking at things from multiple viewpoints.

Skill: *Develop and maintain a clear vision for your organization and the long-term, big-picture needs and opportunities that support the vision.*

Actions: • Ask yourself if you can really articulate what "vision" means to you, and what *your* vision is for the company.
               • Identify what makes your vision exciting and inspiring to you.
               • Write down your vision, and be as specific as possible. What do the products and services look like? Who are your customers? What type of people make up your organization? How can you contribute to achieving this vision? What learning and resources need to be acquired to support this vision?

Skill: *Create an aspirational statement.*

Actions: • Develop a vision that challenges the entire organization.
               • Describe the ideal end state for the organization.
               • Ask yourself, "What are the headlines I would like to read five years from now that would describe the state of our business?"

Skill: *Create an inspirational statement.*

Actions: • Develop a vision that reflects the values of your employees and that motivates them to perform at their highest levels.
               • Ask yourself, "Would I want to have my picture taken next to this vision statement?"

Skill: *Describe the ideal end state.*

Actions: • Expand measures of success.
               • Write down what success would look like to you at the end of five years.
               • Ask yourself, "How will I know we have been successful?"

Leadership Competency 14: Communicating the Vision

Skill:	*Anticipate the values of your audience.*
Action:	• Assess who your audience is going to be and what their values are. Find the connection between your vision and their values.

Skill:	*Write the headline.*
Action:	• Ask the audience to write headline and lead paragraph for a newspaper article about their company that might be written five years from now.

Skill:	*Develop scenarios for your team five years out.*
Actions:	• Develop long-range goals for yourself: Define the goal, set milestones, and define outcome standards. • Then, in addition, determine the attitudes, knowledge, and skill sets that will help you achieve these goals.

Skill:	*Provide employees with the department's vision statement and objectives.*
Actions:	• Provide every employee (including new hires) with a copy of the department's vision statement and objectives, and make sure each person's role in meeting these is clear. • Practice communicating the company's vision to co-workers and customers.

Skill:	*Talk to others about communication breakdowns.*
Actions:	• Talk with peers and people in other departments about any breakdown in communication as soon as they happen. • Devise ways to avoid them. • Analyze the core processes in your business, and identify the critical communication touch-points.

Leadership Competency 15:
Strategic Planning

Skill: *Conduct an environmental scan.*

Actions: • Analyze the environmental factors that might affect the strategic plan (e.g., the economy, the marketplace, the competition, demographic changes, etc.).
               • Ask yourself, "Have we considered all the internal and external factors that might affect the business?"

Skill: *Define the strategic planning process.*

Actions: • Set dates for each phase of the planning process.
               • Let people know when their revenue and expense predictions are due, as well as deadlines for their "people" and program plans.
               • Monitor progress on the plan so that you are sure you will be able to complete it before the fiscal year begins and still have time for people to complete their individual performance plans.

Skill: *Create a vision statement.*

Actions: • Describe the ideal end state.
               • Define what success looks like five years out.
               • Create a statement that is both aspirational and inspirational.
               • Ask yourself, "Would I like to have my picture taken next to this vision statement?"

Skill: *Create a mission statement.*

Actions: • Describe the nature of the work. Define what you are going to do for whom.
               • Ask yourself, "Does this statement adequately describe our purpose?"

Skill: *Develop goals.*

Actions: • Create goals to support the mission.
               • Develop goals for people, products, programs, policies, processes, technology, culture, and finance.
               • Ask yourself, "Do these goals adequately capture our direction for the future?"

Skill: *Set objectives.*

Actions: • Write SMART objectives for each of the goals (**s**pecific, **m**easurable, **a**chievable, **r**atable, and **t**ime-bound).
               • Create 1–5 scales for each of the objectives: 1 stand for *an unacceptable outcome;* 3 stands for *an acceptable outcome;* and 5 stands for *the ideal outcome.*

(continued)

Leadership Competency 15:
Strategic Planning *(concluded)*

Skill: *Define tasks.*

Actions:
- Write monthly tasks for each objective.
- Project tasks only for three months at a time.
- Review the tasks quarterly in order to evaluate progress.
- Ask yourself, "Have we allocated sufficient resources to be successful?"

Skill: *Articulate the product strategy.*

Actions:
- Clarify the strategy for your products, services, and solutions.
- Identify which products are innovative, commercial, or commoditized.
- Ask yourself, "Are we being realistic about how much time it will take for our new products, services, and solutions to get to market?"

Skill: *Articulate the market strategy.*

Actions:
- Identify which verticals you will address and the amount of resources you will allocate.
- Identify the market size you will go after.
- List the specific customers with whom you expect to have the most success.

Skill: *Articulate the distribution strategy.*

Actions:
- Identify which distribution channels you will be leveraging for each market in each vertical.
- Do a cost analysis on direct sales, indirect sales, and channel partners.
- Ask yourself, "Are we using the most cost-effective distribution strategy for each market?"

Leadership Competency 16:
Setting Goals

Skill: *Develop goals.*

Actions:
- Create goals to support the mission.
- Develop goals for people, products, programs, policies, processes, technology, culture, and finance.
- Ask yourself, "Do these goals adequately capture our direction for the future?"

Skill: *Analyze and prioritize your work priorities.*

Actions:
- Analyze your work on a weekly basis and determine your priorities for the week. Then, on a daily basis, plan in detail the work you want to complete that day.
- Allow time each day for planning and thinking. Plan the next day's activities at the end of each day.

Skill: *Create a learning and development plan.*

Action:
- Create a learning and development plan: In your plan, list goals/objectives, resources required, and dates (negotiate these with your manager).

Skill: *Develop methods for keeping track of your work and your promises.*

Action:
- Establish methods for keeping track of your work and your promises (e.g., set personal deadlines, record due dates and appointments in a time management calendar, etc.).

Skill: *Talk to peers and your management team about their goals and concerns.*

Actions:
- Informally talk with your peers and your management team about their goals and concerns.
- Use this information when you need to link your ideas to their needs.

Skill: *Collaborate with other colleagues to keep one another accountable.*

Actions:
- Meet regularly with colleagues to discuss goals and accomplishments.
- Find ways to support one another's growth and progress.
- Help each person generate solutions and strategies that move him/her closer to achieving personal goals.

Leadership Competency 17:
Setting Objectives

Skill:	*Break large projects into several small steps with specific deadlines.*
Actions:	• Track completion of each step to ensure the success of the plan. • Involve those affected by a plan in the creation of the plan.

Skill:	*Develop methods for keeping track of your work and promises.*
Actions:	• Establish methods for keeping track of your work and promises (e.g., set personal deadlines, record due dates and appointments in a time management calendar, etc.). • Develop measurements for the implementation of new products and services.

Skill:	*Establish clear standards and performance expectations.*
Actions:	• Establish clear standards and performance expectations with team members. • When faced with internal barriers, devote dedicated time to plan how to overcome these barriers.

Skill:	*Evaluate the consequences of your plans.*
Actions:	• At least once a year, evaluate the consequences of your plans with an eye toward spotting trends. See if you underestimated timelines, failed to provide adequate project resources, made assumptions that turned out to be wrong, etc. • Take action to address any issues you have identified. If deadlines are missed, find out why, and incorporate your learning into the next project plan.

Skill:	*Identify assumptions that may cause major problems.*
Actions:	• Identify assumptions underlying your direction or planning efforts that will cause major problems if they turn out to be wrong. • Identify the critical constraints to executing the plan. • Develop strategies to deal with the constraints.

Skill:	*Prioritize what is important and what you want to achieve.*
Actions:	• Spend time prioritizing what is important and what results you would like to achieve. • Identify the critical path to achieving your goals.

Skill:	*Review your business goals to see if your activities are aligned.*
Action:	• Constantly review your business goals to see if your activities are aligned.

(continued)

Leadership Competency 17:
Setting Objectives *(concluded)*

Skill:	*Start with the corporate and organizational goals.*
Actions:	• Always begin departmental objective setting by reviewing the corporate vision, mission, goals, and strategic objectives.
	• If possible, review the high-level goals for all organizations to determine if there are interdependencies that may require your attention.
	• Ask yourself, "Am I clear about the strategic direction and how I can contribute to that?"

Skill:	*Specify the desired result.*
Actions:	• Write down your measures of success.
	• What are your departmental goals?
	• Ask yourself, "How will I know when I've been successful?"
	• Make sure your goals are aligned with and support corporate goals.

Skill:	*Develop a scale to rate the objective.*
Action:	• Create a five-point scale that describes the range of possible outcomes. Make level 5 the *ideal* outcome and level 1 the *totally unacceptable* outcome. Make level 3 the *acceptable* outcome.

Skill:	*Make sure that the objective is achievable.*
Actions:	• Show your scales to your team and your colleagues.
	• Ask them if they think that level 3 is the appropriate level to shoot for, and whether or not they think level 3 is achievable.

Skill:	*Set time and budget limits.*
Actions:	• Estimate time and resources for each objective.
	• Clarify who is responsible for what steps, and by what date.
	• Ask yourself, "Have we allocated sufficient resources to achieve these objectives?"

Leadership Competency 18:
Planning and Organizing

Skill: *Analyze and prioritize your work priorities.*

Action: • Analyze your work on a weekly basis, and determine your priorities for
               the week. Plan in detail the work you want to complete each day.

Skill: *Involve others in planning.*

Actions: • After developing a plan, ask your team or a trusted colleague to identify
                 potential problems.
               • Ask everyone involved in the plan to assess how realistic it is.
               • Ask yourself how you will ensure commitment to the plan.
               • Consider involving customers/suppliers in the planning process.

Skill: *Identify the major constraints to executing the plan.*

Actions: • List all the resources and supplies that will be required to implement a plan.
               • Consider any gaps or needs that may be difficult to fulfill.
               • Identify the different ways certain resources may be obtained or obstacles
                 may be overcome.
               • Determine what acceptable substitutes or solutions exist.

Skill: *Monitor plans and follow up on progress.*

Actions: • Establish systems that enable you to measure and monitor progress.
               • Ask people to write down action steps, and agree on when specifically you
                 will follow up with them on progress.
               • Update your progress by checking off completed tasks or phases once they
                 are completed, highlighting for yourself and others the progress you are
                 making toward the final goal.

Leadership Competency 19:
Resource Planning

Skill: *Encourage the team to gather information/benchmarking to make better decisions.*

Action:
- In preparation for making a major decision, encourage the team to gather information and/or benchmarks from at least three sources before making an off-the-cuff decision.

Skill: *Evaluate business and financial data you regularly receive.*

Actions:
- Evaluate all of the business and financial data you regularly receive (electronically or otherwise), and make it available to your team within the limits of confidentiality guidelines.
- Ask team members what information they would like to have in order to do their jobs better. If it is not available, find out how to obtain it on a regular basis.

Skill: *Gain exposure to a major business issue or initiative.*

Action:
- Perform in a role that provides exposure to a major business issue or change initiative (e.g., a new system, a major development effort, an organizational start-up, or a major reorganization).

Skill: *Integrate organizational structures/processes/workforce issues.*

Action:
- Work with the business team leader and his/her team at the highest levels to integrate organizational structures, processes, and workforce issues into the business equation.

Skill: *Lead an effort that involves a major structural realignment.*

Action:
- Lead an effort that involves a major structural realignment (e.g., start-up, significant growth, downsizing, plant closing, restructuring, business turnaround, acquisition, partnership).

Skill: *Lead an organization that supports one or more businesses.*

Action:
- Lead an organization that supports one or more businesses through activities such as establishing effective communication with the business teams, developing methodologies and procedures, and creating a positive internal and external team environment.

Skill: *Negotiate an important partnership.*

Action:
- Perform in a role that requires you to negotiate important parts of a partnership that make a significant financial impact on the overall business (e.g., developing practices or procedures that produce significant improvements in cost, quality, cycle time, or productivity).

Leadership Competency 20:
Developing a Business Plan

Skill:　　　*Analyze marketing and sales effectiveness.*

Actions:
- Review regularly how well your marketing and sales investments are meeting business objectives.
- Analyze revenue per salesperson, taking into account differences in market and geographic regions.
- Ask yourself, "Are my marketing efforts generating the demand I would expect? Is my sales team achieving superior productivity, compared with competitors?"

Skill:　　　*Target high-potential areas.*

Actions:
- Analyze vertical and horizontal markets for the best opportunities.
- Determine which geographies represent the best potential for sales.
- Target specific market segments.

Skill:　　　*Allocate resources.*

Actions:
- Distribute your human and financial capital based on performance and potential.
- Ask yourself, "Am I allocating resources in ways that give the organization the best chance for sustainable return on investment?"

Skill:　　　*Set short-term and long-term targets.*

Actions:
- Develop specific, measurable, achievable, ratable, and time-bound goals and objectives.
- Set targets for each month, each quarter, and each year.
- Project targets over a 3–5 year time period, and revisit them each year.

Skill:　　　*Develop solution strategies.*

Actions:
- Create solutions that respond to market demand.
- Ask customers what they want and need.
- Ask yourself, "Can I build a better, faster, cheaper solution than my competition?"
- Most importantly, ask yourself, "How is my solution different, and what is the economic model for it?"

Skill:　　　*Develop distribution strategies.*

Actions:
- Identify the most cost-effective ways to distribute your products, services, and solutions.
- Ask yourself, "For each market segment and vertical, what distribution strategy makes the most sense (i.e., direct, channel, indirect, partner)?"

(continued)

Leadership Competency 20:
Developing a Business Plan *(concluded)*

Skill: *Develop a financial plan.*

Actions:
- Calculate your fixed costs, cost of sales, overhead, break-even point, and sales forecast.
- Develop your balance sheet, cash flow sheet, and income statement.

Skill: *Create an action plan.*

Actions:
- Develop specific, measurable, achievable, ratable, and time-bound goals and objectives.
- Assign who will do what for each objective and task.
- Create task cards each month that identify who is responsible for what steps and by which dates.
- Estimate time and resource requirements for each step.

Leadership Competency 21:
Setting Priorities

Skill:	*Identify all the objectives you need to accomplish.*
Actions:	• Write down all the tasks and projects you are responsible for.
	• Estimate the amount of time you think it will take to complete each task.
	• Ask yourself, "Are there any tasks I can eliminate from this list or delegate to others?"

Skill:	*Identify the most urgent objectives.*
Actions:	• Assign weights to each item on your list: 1 = *not at all urgent* and 5 = *extremely urgent.*
	• Group them by urgency, with the most urgent at the top.

Skill:	*Identify the most important objectives.*
Actions:	• Assign weights to each item on your list: 1 = *not at all important* and 5 = *critically important.*
	• Group them by importance, with the most important at the top.

Skill:	*Select the most important and urgent objectives as priorities.*
Actions:	• Create a 2 × 2 grid. Write "Urgency" on the vertical axis and "Importance" on the horizontal axis.
	• Map your list of objectives into the grid, using the ratings you applied as you weighted each for importance and urgency.
	• Circle the items that are extremely urgent AND critically important.
	• Ask yourself, "Am I applying my time and energy appropriately to these items?"

Skill:	*Review the grid once per month to measure progress on the priorities and to see if priorities have changed.*
Actions:	• Add items in each column during the month and rate them on the urgency and importance scale.
	• Place them in your grid.
	• At the end of each month, determine which items you can remove from the grid and which priorities have changed.

Section 4—Making the Hard Decisions

Leadership Competency 22	Restructuring
Leadership Competency 23	Recruiting the Right Talent
Leadership Competency 24	Process Analysis
Leadership Competency 25	Process Design and Mapping

Leadership Competency 22: Restructuring

Skill: *Lead an effort that involves a major structural realignment.*

Action:
- Lead an effort that involves a major structural realignment (e.g., start-up, significant growth, downsizing, plant closings, restructuring, business turnaround, acquisition, or partnership).

Skill: *Work on a project to rebuild a customer relationship.*

Action:
- Participate in addressing a difficult situation in which the company's reputation is in jeopardy by helping rebuild customer relationships and realigning or restructuring product/service delivery.

Skill: *Dispose of non-performing assets.*

Actions:
- Evaluate the profit and loss statements of each of your businesses.
- Ask yourself, "What are the costs and benefits of keeping this division or function?" If you determine that the asset does not have the potential to perform, consider disposing of it unless there are compelling counter-balancing reasons.

Skill: *Expand to respond to an opportunity.*

Actions:
- Continuously search for the marketplace that holds new opportunities.
- Ask yourself, "Is this a niche we could capture?"
- Create a business case for the new opportunity.
- Invest in the resources required to make it a success.

Skill: *Re-position, based on market changes.*

Actions:
- Scan the environment for changes that could affect you.
- Study the competition, the economy, and the marketplace.
- See changes as opportunities to re-position yourself with new products, new markets, or new distribution strategies.

(continued)

Leadership Competency 22:
Restructuring *(concluded)*

Skill: *Align capabilities behind the new positioning.*

Actions:
- After you have defined what your positioning is, what it does, and why it will yield positive results, align your individual and organizational capabilities behind the positioning.
- Ask yourself, "Do I have the right people, the right processes, and the right technology to capitalize on this positioning?"

Skill: *Downsize to cut operating expenses.*

Actions:
- Monitor revenue and expense trends carefully.
- If expenses are starting to exceed revenues and you don't see a way to reverse the trend, consider reducing expenses.
- If you have to lay off employees, make sure it is done with respect, integrity, and fairness.

Skill: *Merge with or acquire another company.*

Actions:
- Study changes in the marketplace.
- Look for companies that could complement what your company does and strengthen your positioning.
- If you do decide to merge, pay as much attention to the people and cultural issues as you do to the financial issues.
- Create a transition team, and dedicate high-level talent to making sure the transition goes well.

Skill: *Issue a "tracking stock."*

Actions:
- Identify portions of your business that can be tracked separately in order to determine value.
- Issue a stock for that segment of the company under the protection of the parent.
- Track the value.

Leadership Competency 23:
Recruiting the Right Talent

Skill: *Develop a workforce requirements plan.*

Actions:
- Identify business requirements for the future.
- Determine how those requirements will create new demands for the organization.
- Identify the competencies required to meet those demands.
- Project hiring needs over the next few years.
- Develop a plan to meet those needs.

Skill: *Use multiple sourcing methods.*

Actions:
- Optimize Internet recruiting and broker internal talent.
- Use social networks to do direct recruiting.
- Tap diverse sources, including professional associations and universities.
- Reward employees who make good referrals.

Skill: *Assess candidates.*

Actions:
- Use an applicant tracking system for initial assessment.
- Narrow the list of candidates by using well-defined predictors of performance excellence.
- Assess functional and technical capabilities, as well as cultural fit, experience, and past performance.
- Use assessment centers to simulate real-life job challenges.

Skill: *Make a compelling offer.*

Actions:
- Address the candidate's key concerns and questions.
- Offer a package that includes compensation, benefits, and career opportunities.
- Match corporate values with the individual's values.
- Explain the economic and social value of accepting the job.
- Articulate the career value proposition.

Skill: *Engage the new employees quickly and effectively.*

Actions:
- Orient the new colleague to the organizational strategy, structure, and culture.
- Build a relationship between the new hire and the organization, and facilitate connections with key resources.
- Train the new person on the technologies necessary to work effectively.
- Make your new colleague aware of their options for career development.

Leadership Competency 24:
Process Analysis

Skill: *Commit to methods for keeping track of your work and your promises.*

Actions: • Establish methods for keeping track of your work and your promises
              (e.g., set personal deadlines, record due dates and appointments in a
              time-management calendar, etc.).
              • Develop measurements that track achievements vs. initial goals.

Skill: *Use process mapping.*

Action: • Learn how to do process mapping and process analysis, and apply
              the techniques as appropriate in your setting.

Skill: *Use quality principles and techniques.*

Actions: • Learn quality principles, such as Six Sigma.
              • Use process analysis, mapping, and modeling techniques on every
              project to enhance the value of the project.

Skill: *Spend time with your team analyzing current problems/opportunities.*

Action: • Identify which key behaviors you should start, stop, or continue in order to
              improve process performance.

Skill: *Use project management software.*

Actions: • Use project management software (such as Microsoft Project) to develop
              project plans, commitments, deliverables, timelines, etc.
              • Use collaborative software for shared information (e.g., calendars).

Leadership Competency 25:
Process Design and Mapping

Skill:	*Select the right process to map.*
Actions:	• Expand the list of processes that are used in your department. • Ask yourself, "Which processes are core to the business?" • Select the most-critical process that has the biggest impact on the business.

Skill:	*Identify team members and responsibilities.*
Actions:	• Involve a cross-functional team in the project to re-design a process or create a process map. • Invite team members who are directly or indirectly affected by the process. • Clarify expectations and timelines.

Skill:	*Map the process.*
Actions:	• Make the work visible by creating a flowchart. • Identify where decisions are made and make sure there is clear authority for the decisions. • Illustrate the sequence of events and how work flows.

Skill:	*Analyze the process.*
Actions:	• Review the map and identify bottlenecks, sources of delay, errors being fixed vs. errors prevented, role ambiguity, duplications, unnecessary steps, and cycle time. • Change the process map to address any problems you have identified.

Skill:	*Identify measures of success.*
Actions:	• Consider metrics in the areas of customer satisfaction, organizational performance, supplier satisfaction, financial improvement, and employee satisfaction. • Choose those metrics for which accurate and complete data is available; metrics that don't cause people to act in ways that are contrary to the business; and metrics that are simple and SMART. • Ask yourself, "Are these measures driving us to do the right thing?"

Skill:	*Document and deploy the "to-be" process.*
Actions:	• After you have mapped and analyzed the process, develop an implementation plan. • Review progress on the plan at regular intervals. • Ask yourself, "How are we doing on our measures of success?"

Chapter 2: Building
The Second Meta-Competency

Introduction

Leadership is more than identifying opportunities, threats, strategies, and people.

- **Great leaders also build the teams, the processes, and the technologies needed to capitalize on the opportunities, mitigate the threats, and implement the strategy.**

- **While it is important to articulate the vision, mission, values, and current reality, it is equally important to build the capabilities required for success.**

In that regard, this chapter has four sections:

Section 1   Building Individual Capabilities
Section 2   Building Team Capabilities
Section 3   Building Organizational Capabilities
Section 4   Building Customer Relationships and Capabilities

Building individual capabilities is all about knowing and growing yourself and others. A great leader must have an objective assessment of his or her strengths and weaknesses, and make an effort to grow. Effective leaders also develop talent within the organization. This means knowing and growing others. Leaders are committed to developing themselves and others.

Building team capabilities means developing high-performing teams. Years of research have demonstrated that teams go through the stages of forming, storming, norming, and performing. Great leaders pay attention to each stage of team development, and take action to elevate performance as the team moves through each stage. Effective leaders spend time developing their employees and their teams, establishing strong connections, and creating a sense of community.

Building organizational capabilities means *knowing and growing the business*. Great leaders understand marketplace requirements and develop the organizational capabilities to respond quickly and effectively to changes in conditions. Organizational capabilities include decision making, planning, process engineering, product development, and communication. Building these capabilities requires an engaged and empowered workforce that knows how to capitalize on opportunities and provide high-quality solutions to meet customer needs.

Building customer relationships means *knowing the people* who buy your products, services, and solutions and building and nurturing your relationships with them. Great leaders elevate the relationships with their customers, moving from the role of vendor to the role of a trusted advisor. Customers now demand an interdependent partnership with suppliers in which each party seeks ways to help the other grow. Effective leaders mobilize their teams around the commitment to help customers grow.

Section I—Building Individual Capabilities

Leadership Competency 26	Personal Development
Leadership Competency 27	Building Emotional Intelligence
Leadership Competency 28	Identifying Paradigm Shifts (Building Paradigms)
Leadership Competency 29	Building Effective Relationships
Leadership Competency 30	Business Acumen
Leadership Competency 31	Coaching
Leadership Competency 32	Collaborating
Leadership Competency 33	Communicating Openly and Effectively
Leadership Competency 34	Influencing
Leadership Competency 35	Interviewing
Leadership Competency 36	Listening
Leadership Competency 37	Consulting Effectively
Leadership Competency 38	Giving and Receiving Feedback
Leadership Competency 39	Being Honest
Leadership Competency 40	Mentoring
Leadership Competency 41	Presenting
Leadership Competency 42	Practicing Business Etiquette
Leadership Competency 43	Business Writing
Leadership Competency 44	Building Cognitive Skills

Leadership Competency 26: Personal Development

Skill: *Identify personal goals.*

Actions:
- Explore where you want to be in your life and in your career in the next five years.
- Set objectives for living, learning, and working.
- Ask yourself, "Where do I need to be at the end of one year in each of these three areas to give me a sense of confidence that I am making good progress toward my goals?"

Skill: *Identify competencies required to reach those goals.*

Actions:
- For each of your living, learning, and working objectives, investigate the competencies required for success. For example, you may need to enhance your interpersonal relating competency to achieve your living and working goals.
- Identify three competency requirements in each area.

Skill: *Assess yourself on the competencies.*

Actions:
- For each of the competencies you identified, do a self-assessment and ask a friend or colleague to do an assessment of you. Use a 1–5 scale for the assessment, with 1 being *not at all proficient* and 5 being *totally proficient.*
- Assess where you are and where you think you need to be on the scales.

(continued)

Leadership Competency 26:
Personal Development *(concluded)*

Skill: *Create a development plan to close the gaps between where you are and where you need to be.*

Actions:
- For each competency on which there is a gap between current proficiency and required proficiency, develop an improvement plan.
- Set milestones, and make each step small enough to be achievable.
- Identify how you will reward yourself for reaching your milestones.

Skill: *Identify and build the support you will need to implement your plan.*

Actions:
- Increase your probability for success by joining a support group or asking a friend or mentor to join you and/or support you.
- Ask yourself, "When I have been most successful in the past, what kind of support did I have?"

Skill: *Measure progress once every month.*

Actions:
- Set aside one day each month to review how well you are doing on your commitments.
- Do a self-assessment, and also ask a friend or colleague to give you feedback.
- Consider joining a support group in which progress reviews are built into the process.

Skill: *Reward yourself for achieving your goals.*

Actions:
- Think about your biggest motivators.
- Expand the list.
- Choose rewards for goal achievement that are commensurate with the effort.

Leadership Competency 27:
Building Emotional Intelligence

Skill: *Assess organizational needs.*

Actions:
- Determine the competencies that are the most critical for effective performance in a particular type of job.
- Use a valid method, such as comparing of the behavioral-event interviews of superior performers to those of average performers.
- Make sure the competencies are congruent with the organization's culture and strategy.

Skill: *Assess the individual.*

Actions:
- Use multiple sources of data to assess the key competencies needed for a particular job.
- Assess all aspects of emotional intelligence (e.g., ability to relate well to all people, the ability to build a team, cultural sensitivity, etc.).

Skill: *Conduct assessments with care.*

Actions:
- Give the individual information about his/her strengths and weaknesses.
- Allow time for the person to digest and integrate the information.
- Provide the feedback in a safe and supportive environment in order to minimize resistance and defensiveness.

Skill: *Maximize learner choice.*

Actions:
- Allow people to decide whether or not they will participate in the development process.
- Have them set their own change goals.

Skill: *Encourage participation.*

Actions:
- Provide support for developmental opportunities.
- Promote multiple ways to access learning (e.g., Web-based training, classroom, e-learning, self-paced, seminars, etc.).

Skill: *Link learning goals to personal values.*

Actions:
- Help people understand whether or not a given change fits with what matters most to them.
- Ask yourself, "Does this change fit with this person's values and hopes?"

Leadership Competency 28:
Identifying Paradigm Shifts (Building Paradigms)

Skill: *Identify existing and new components of paradigms.*

Actions: • Challenge assumptions around the components of a particular solution. For example, does transportation consist of trains and cars, or could it include planes and space travel?
               • Ask yourself if your view of the components of a solution could limit the possibilities.
               • Read Thomas Kuhn's book, *The Structure of Scientific Revolution.*

Skill: *Identify existing and new functions of paradigms.*

Actions: • Challenge assumptions around the functions of a particular solution. For example, does collaboration consist of connecting and communicating? Or could it include cooperation and co-orchestration?
               • Ask yourself if your view of the functions of a solution might limit the possibilities.

Skill: *Identify existing and new processes of paradigms.*

Actions: • Investigate how anything from business to day-to-day events were done in a particular area, and how, through creativity and innovation, the processes have taken a giant leap (e.g., typewriters to computers).
               • Ask yourself if your view of the processes or research techniques behind a solution might limit the possibilities.
               • Explore new theoretical pathways.

Skill: *Identify existing and new conditions of paradigms.*

Actions: • Challenge assumptions around the conditions required to successfully implement a solution. For example, does communication consist of informing people? Or can it include involving, incorporating, or inspiring people? Does work get done by controlling mechanisms? Or by freeing mechanisms?
               • Ask yourself if your view of the conditions required for success might limit the possibilities.

Skill: *Identify existing and new standards of paradigms.*

Actions: • Challenge assumptions around the standards required for success. For example, do standards of evidence come from only one source? Or do they incorporate multiple sources? To further clarify, does the standard of evidence for performance management come only from a manager? Or does it come from peers, customers, and subordinates?
               • Ask yourself if your view of standards of measurement might limit the possibilities.

Leadership Competency 29:
Building Effective Relationships

Skill: *Identify your strengths, weaknesses, learning style, management style, and conflict style.*

Action:
- Take a personality test (e.g., Myers Briggs Type Inventory) to understand your own personality style and that of others, and how it affects your success and the team.

Skill: *Respond with appropriate concern to co-workers' issues.*

Actions:
- Be aware of times when co-workers are hurting in their personal lives (e.g., death, illness, divorce, etc.). Express your interest and concern in words, by a visit, with an appropriate card, or with a gift of flowers.
- Listen to what they are expressing to you, and show that you understand their feelings and values.

Skill: *Show respect for others' values and beliefs.*

Actions:
- When another person is talking, listen carefully to hear his or her values and beliefs.
- Check out your understanding respectfully and non-confrontationally, even if the values you hear are very different from your own. A value is anything that is important to another person. For example, physically a person may value privacy; emotionally, a person may value teamwork; intellectually, a person may value challenge; spiritually, a person may value connectedness.

Skill: *Build a personal network of contacts to help solve problems.*

Actions:
- Take personal initiative to build a network of contacts with whom you can identify and solve problems and define potential problems, vulnerabilities, and opportunities with product and service offerings. This network could be a community of practice or a community of interest in which people come together to work on areas of similar interests.
- Develop a systematic approach to networking. Analyze what you need in a network, and what you can offer other members.

Skill: *Seek to understand differences.*

Actions:
- Carefully monitor the way in which you seek understanding of differences.
- Be open and willing to explain your desire to learn, rather than push too quickly for resolution.
- Follow the process of exploration, understanding, and action.
- Spending sufficient time in exploration increases your chances of understanding accurately and thoroughly.
- Build on areas of agreement before you address areas of difference.
- Acknowledge the points on which you agree before you state the points on which you disagree.

(continued)

Leadership Competency 29:
Building Effective Relationships *(continued)*

Skill: *Check the clarity of all your communications.*

Actions: • Check the clarity of all your communications by asking others to summarize what you've said and what they think you meant.
                • Use a give-get-merge-go format to clarify communications. This means **giving** your perspective, **getting** their image of the situation, **merging** images, and deciding how to **go** forward.

Skill: *Find solutions that work for all involved.*

Action: • When resolving differences or a conflict, begin by clearly stating your desire to find a solution that will work for all involved. A solution that works for all involved is one that satisfies many or most of all parties' values.

Skill: *Confront problems, not people.*

Actions: • Problems or issues include a person's behavior, process inefficiency, technology malfunction, cultural norms, product problems, or a lack of knowledge.
                • If a person's behavior needs to be addressed, be specific with facts and how the behavior is affecting relationships or progress.
                • If you have to confront a person about their behavior, remember that tone is often more important than content.
                • Confronting a person about their behavior should be done respectfully.

Skill: *Create a clear vision of the kind of leader you want to be.*

Action: • Effective leaders identify opportunities and threats, build teamwork and programs, and drive for results. Your vision should include a combination of all three of these primary functions.

Skill: *Define "conflict" in terms of needs, not solutions.*

Actions: • People may disagree about the right solution, but they can *agree* on which values are important in order to focus on creative problem solving and the search for alternatives.
                • De-personalize the conflict.
                • Catch yourself when you fall into the trap of believing that the other person is deliberately trying to make the situation difficult for you.

(continued)

Leadership Competency 29:
Building Effective Relationships *(continued)*

Skill:	*Develop these "helping skills" in your everyday relationships.*
Actions:	• *Attending:* leaning toward the other person and listening attentively. • *Responding:* expressing empathy and accurately paraphrasing feeling and meaning. • *Personalizing:* responding to feeling and meaning, helping the other person identify his or her role in a problem, and forming a goal. • *Initiating:* sharing specific steps for developing an initiative or achieving the goal.
Skill:	*Don't "catastrophize" events at work.*
Actions:	• Problems are to be expected, and they are rarely catastrophic. Exaggerating problems and focusing on the negative drains your own energy and the energy of others. • Expect change, ambiguity, and frustration—at least part of the time.
Skill:	*Don't personalize disagreements.*
Action:	• See conflict as a disagreement about goals, values, ideas, or methods. Don't think of it as a conflict of personality or style. Disagreements that are seen as personality or style conflicts become more difficult to resolve.
Skill:	*Create a climate of trust.*
Actions:	• Make sure you are not manipulating. • Don't manipulate people or create a climate of mistrust around you. • In particular, don't use information unfairly to gain advantage. For example, do what you say, say what you do, be genuine in what you say, and stay focused on what you do. • Stand behind your employees and back their decisions. Support in public, criticize in private.
Skill:	*Explain why others should consider your point of view.*
Action:	• Openly acknowledge it when your opinion or perspective is unpopular, and then explain why it is important for others to consider why you have chosen your point of view.

(continued)

Leadership Competency 29:
Building Effective Relationships *(continued)*

Skill: *Give people the feedback they need, even when it is difficult.*

Actions: • Remember, people tend to listen to those who have listened to them.
               • Before presenting your feedback, decide whether and when it should
                 be given.
               • Avoid using words and tones that are antagonizing and that will block
                 your message from getting through.
               • Focus on people's good qualities, rather than on their deficiencies. While
                 it is sometimes necessary to point out deficits that are hindering growth
                 and/or progress, it is important to provide balanced feedback whenever
                 possible.

Skill: *Meet face-to-face with global team members.*

Actions: • Plan more face-to-face interactions with global team members early in your
                 relationship.
               • Choose carefully what meetings need to be face-to-face and what meetings
                 can be done through e-rooms, video conferencing, tele-conferencing, or
                 Web-x/placeware.
               • Make sure you gear the content to the format. For example, if you are just
                 sharing information, an e-room will work well.
               • If you are brainstorming critical issues, then face-to-face may be more
                 appropriate.

Skill: *Provide motivation to others to resolve their differences.*

Actions: • Provide motivation for people involved in ongoing or recurring conflict
                 to resolve their differences. Motivation depends on the level of functioning
                 and values of the people.
               • Assess their level of functioning (detractor, observer, participant, contributor,
                 or leader) and understand the respective values as input for your motiva-
                 tional strategy.

Skill: *Report on your successes and your failures with equal candor.*

Actions: • Review successes, especially when you are going through a challenging time.
               • Write down your strengths, achievements, and what's working well on a
                 regular basis.

Skill: *Seek understanding of the other person's point of view.*

Actions: • Summarize what you hear until the other person agrees that you understand
                 what he or she thinks and feels.
               • Show respect for employees' ideas and experiences by asking for their input,
                 advice, and involvement.

(continued)

Leadership Competency 29:
Building Effective Relationships *(concluded)*

Skill: *Solicit feedback about the impact of your activities on others.*

Action: • Actively solicit information regarding how your activities and projects are impacting others (positively and negatively).

Skill: *Delegate activities to team members.*

Actions: • Start delegating more activities to team members. Delegation depends on the commitment and capabilities of the person to whom the work is being delegated, as well as the organizational support for the work.
  • Based on the levels of commitment, capability, and support within the organizational culture, leaders can decide how much support, direction, and coaching is required for the person to be successful.

Skill: *Think before responding in pressure situations.*

Action: • Build in the discipline of thinking before responding in pressure situations. This gives you time to calm down, think of alternatives, and see things in other ways.

Leadership Competency 30:
Business Acumen

Skill: *Clarify the business value of opportunities or strategies.*

Action: • Proactively clarify the "business value" of specific opportunities or strategies with team members (e.g., ROI, margins, business impact).

Skill: *Get help from content experts.*

Action: • Get help from a financial/budget professional to help you set up budget templates (i.e., Excel, etc.) to track the financial progress of your projects.

Skill: *Lead a large project involving multiple teams.*

Actions: • Lead a large project that includes the forming of multiple but integrated teams, clarifying and facilitating the performance of responsibilities with team leaders and negotiating and coordinating significant resources.
• Lead an organization that supports one or more businesses that include such activities as establishing effective communications with the business teams, developing methodologies and procedures, and creating a positive internal and external team environment.

Skill: *Lead an effort that involves a major structural realignment.*

Action: • Lead an effort that involves a major structural realignment (e.g., start-up, significant growth, downsizing, plant closings, restructuring, business turnaround, acquisition, or partnership).

Skill: *Identify resource requirements when developing plans.*

Action: • When developing plans, make lists of the resource requirements and compare to similar projects. Also review and analyze differences and similarities. Resource requirements could include people, dollars, time, space, management support, etc.

Skill: *Develop specific action plans for each project.*

Actions: • Make sure there are specific action plans for each project that supports a business objective, and track milestones frequently.
• Use the 5WH method: **Who** is doing **what**? **Where** and **when** is the work supposed to be done? **Why** is the work important? **How** will results be measured?

(continued)

Leadership Competency 30:
Business Acumen *(concluded)*

Skill: *Reality-test all plans with your team.*

Actions: • Reality-test all plans with your team. Brainstorm anything that could
                 go wrong.
               • Ask your team four important questions:
                 — Do we have sufficient commitment?
                 — Do we have adequate capabilities?
                 — Do we have cultural and leadership support for this plan?
                 — Do we have the right people, the right process, and the right technology
                   to enable this plan?

Leadership Competency 31:
Coaching

Skill: *Assess your own coaching approach.*

Actions: • Ask yourself what kind of coach you want to be. Think back on important role models or coaches you have had, what you learned from them, and what impact they had on you.
                • Identify what your strengths and weaknesses are as a coach in order to determine who/what you are best suited to coach and what your limitations might be.
                • Who can help you develop skills as a coach?

Skill: *Provide high-impact development opportunities.*

Actions: • Find ways to give your employees assignments that provide important developmental opportunities: representing you at a meeting, leading a cross-functional task force, working or meeting with a senior manager, becoming a mentor to a new or inexperienced employee, and so on.
                • Ask yourself how you can help employees network with the right people and gain access to resources, new skills, and important learning opportunities.

Skill: *Find out what is important to people.*

Actions: • Remember: Coaching does not mean solving people's problems.
                • Listen to the person's needs, concerns, desires, and motivations in order to fully understand who they are and what they want.
                • Ask questions to help the person clarify their own thinking and to gain a fuller sense of his/her thinking, views, and opinions.
                • Suspend your own agenda and suppress your desire to give advice without fully understanding.
                • Find out what excites the person, how they view themselves, and what they believe about their ability to develop.

Skill: *Be a role model for development.*

Actions: • Be open about the areas within yourself that you are working on and what kind of development and learning opportunities you are seeking.
                • Share what you have learned from your mistakes and your successes.
                • Invite feedback and coaching from others.
                • Push yourself out of your own comfort zone by taking risks and experimenting with new approaches.

Skill: *Build a foundation of trust.*

Actions: • Show consistency between your words and your actions by making realistic commitments and following through.
                • Let people know what you expect of them so that they are not caught off guard or confused about their responsibilities and your expectations.
                • Demonstrate that you have their best interests in mind by creating time for them, showing compassion, and listening intently to their needs, concerns, questions, and ideas.

Leadership Competency 32: Collaborating

Skill: *Remove barriers to collaboration.*

Actions:
- Establish clear agendas, ground rules, and team decisions/actions as part of an effective meeting approach.
- Be sure that the goals of all teams are in alignment with the organization's goals.
- Ask yourself whether or not the team has the tools and support it needs to work together effectively. If not, what needs to be done to make sure that the team is on the right track?

Skill: *Discourage "we vs. they" thinking.*

Actions:
- Build teamwork among different groups by identifying a common problem or issue that a cross-functional task force or committee could solve.
- Evaluate your employees on their willingness and ability to work as part of a team, and reach out to others in different departments and functional areas.

Skill: *Build a shared vision and shared goals.*

Actions:
- In order to create a sense of shared vision, involve key stakeholders in building, articulating, and implementing the vision and team goals.
- Make sure everyone has a chance to share ideas and give input to increase commitment and buy-in to the vision and goals.
- Establish accountabilities for achieving shared goals by linking people's responsibilities to the impact on the goal.

Skill: *Build shared values and team norms.*

Actions:
- Agree on a set of behaviors that serve as guidelines for how to perform, interact with one another, make decisions, and accomplish team goals.
- Hold people accountable for behavior by meeting one on one with anyone whose behavior is hurting the group dynamic.
- Create opportunities for team members to acknowledge everyone's strengths and contributions ("What I appreciate about you is . . ." "You really contributed to our goal/team by . . ." "What I wish you would do more of is . . .").

Skill: *Share credit with others.*

Actions:
- Say "we"—not "I."
- Monitor your language in meetings with peers, direct reports, and other company leaders.
- Ask yourself how often you use the word "I" compared with "we."
- How often do you give credit to others when you are singled out and recognized for success?
- When you acknowledge the success of a project, find a way to recognize the effort of all team members involved, no matter how seemingly small their roles or contributions.

(continued)

Leadership Competency 32:
Collaborating *(continued)*

Skill: *Evaluate your effectiveness as a team member.*

Actions: • Become aware of how effectively you currently function as a team member in order to improve your team skills. Do you contribute too much? Too little? What circumstances contribute to your success as a team member?
           • Keep track of the contributions you make and the plans, ideas, or solutions you could have contributed but did not.
           • In order to gain a clearer understanding of your level of effectiveness in team situations, evaluate and determine the reasons behind your performance (such as your preparation, knowledge, interest, comfort level, willingness to listen to others on the team, etc.).

Skill: *Acknowledge the contributions of team members.*

Actions: • Acknowledge, summarize, and reinforce the contributions of your team members.
           • Reinforce through private praise or public recognition. Recognition can take the form of a verbal acknowledgment, a cash award, a promotion, a raise, etc.

Skill: *Adopt a "can-do" attitude and approach to challenges.*

Actions: • Adopt a "can-do" attitude, and approach challenges from a problem-solving perspective.
           • Look for alternative solutions, rather than focus on why things can't be done.
           • Ask yourself, "What are the values and objectives we are trying to achieve? What is the best way to accomplish them?"
           • Avoid prematurely censoring ideas, and don't be concerned about whether or not ideas are flowing in a logical sequence.

Skill: *Review processes on a regular basis.*

Actions: • Ask your business and work teams to review processes on a regular basis.
           • List the three most important processes in your business.
           • Ask your team what is working and what is not working with those processes.
           • Pick one process with high business impact that is not working well.
           • Form a task force to fix it.

Skill: *Communicate openly about process improvements.*

Action: • Communicate to others in the organization about work being done to improve processes. Keeping information about process changes a secret fuels the rumor mill and leads to skepticism and lack of trust.

(continued)

Leadership Competency 32:
Collaborating *(continued)*

Skill: *Determine how you can improve cooperation with other departments.*

Actions:
- Ask people in other departments for input on how your department can be better structured to improve cooperation.
- Determine whether or not you have the information necessary to make a sound decision. If not, decide what you need to know and how you can get the information.
- Encourage cooperation, rather than competition, between different work units.
- Make sure that groups set their goals in harmony with one another, and be sure that the goals are mutually supportive.

Skill: *Conduct training on process flow and continuous improvement.*

Action:
- Include a mini-module on process flow and continuous improvement in initial employee training. This sets the expectation that continuous improvement is an important responsibility, and it also provides some basic skills in process improvement.

Skill: *Develop a network of colleagues.*

Actions:
- Develop a network of colleagues in areas that can help you with planning and organizing projects (i.e., finance, sourcing, etc.).
- Develop a network of cross-functional contacts to tap during project execution.
- Build an informal network of peers in similar organizations through which you can exchange ideas and discuss issues relevant to technical advances in your field.

Skill: *During change, communicate much more frequently.*

Action:
- Remember that when it comes to change, it is almost impossible to communicate too much. People hear things at different times. Therefore, it is necessary to communicate the same message or set of ideas many times and in many different ways for it to be heard and understood.

Skill: *Encourage others to form teams of diverse individuals and skills.*

Actions:
- Encourage others to form teams made up of diverse individuals who represent different functional or business areas. This provides the team with a broader perspective on issues.
- Encourage everyone involved to speak a common language. To avoid alienating outside groups, educate them and help them to understand the "lingo" of the team.

(continued)

Leadership Competency 32:
Collaborating *(continued)*

Skill: *Help team members understand one another better.*

Actions:
- Share information about how work is being done.
- Discuss work histories, specific skills, successes, and talents.
- Help team members to understand, appreciate, and use differences among themselves to arrive at better solutions and to do better work.

Skill: *Include a team performance appraisal as part of the performance management system.*

Action:
- Include an appraisal of team performance, in addition to individual performance, as a part of your performance-management system.

Skill: *Involve employees in setting departmental goals and objectives.*

Actions:
- Track results.
- Recognize and reward employees for their contribution to the success of your team.

Skill: *Use a more participative approach with your decision making.*

Actions:
- Assess your decision-making style and pay attention to the extent to which you solicit others' ideas.
- Ask yourself how many of your decisions are *tell, sell, test, consult,* or *join.*
- Look for opportunities to use a more participative approach.

Skill: *Understand the viewpoint of others.*

Action:
- Be concerned if you are reluctant or unable to understand the viewpoint of others. This reaction is an important warning signal; it will be difficult for you to make a decision that will be received and implemented well if you cannot understand the other points of view (at least partially).

Skill: *Share your expertise and the expertise of others.*

Actions:
- When working with people who pride themselves on their professional expertise, show interest in learning and respect for their knowledge.
- Let them know your areas of expertise and how that might help the business goals.

(continued)

Leadership Competency 32:
Collaborating *(concluded)*

Skill:　　*Use an outside facilitator for important meetings.*

Action:
- When the outcomes of a meeting are particularly important, consider using an outside facilitator. This will allow you to focus on the content of the meeting while the facilitator handles the processes for communication, problem solving, and decision making.

Skill:　　*Use open-ended questions to draw out quieter members of your team.*

Actions:
- Find ways to involve quiet team members without embarrassing them.
- Use open-ended questions to draw out quieter members of your team, and then listen carefully.

Skill:　　*Think interdependently.*

Actions:
- Actively seek ways to help your partners grow and succeed.
- Observe yourself thinking and acting independently and/or competitively.
- For every collaborative relationship in which you participate, ask yourself if it is a "grow-grow" partnership.

Leadership Competency 33:
Communicating Openly and Effectively

Skill: *Adapt your listening behaviors to reflect cultural differences.*

Action:
- If doing business in a different country, be sure to inquire about indigenous communication habits.

Skill: *Address individuals, not a collective group called "the audience."*

Actions:
- Try to personalize your message to the individuals in a group.
- Ask yourself, "Why is this helpful to my listener?"

Skill: *Analyze the costs of pushing your agenda vs. other people's agendas.*

Actions:
- If you "win" this time, will you receive cooperation from the "losers" in the future?
- Think interdependently, instead of only looking for a win for yourself.
- Seek out ways to be helpful to others.
- Ask yourself, "Do I understand fully the other person's agenda?"

Skill: *Anticipate questions, especially tough ones, and prepare strong answers.*

Actions:
- Before any important communication, be prepared to answer questions related to what it is, why it is helpful, how it is done, and/or how often.
- Assess who your audience is going to be and what their "hot buttons" are. Think through how you are going to handle these things so that you appear interested in the audience, yet authoritative.

Skill: *Ask a colleague to signal you whenever you go off the topic at a meeting.*

Action:
- Ask yourself, "Is this something my audience needs to hear? Or is it just something I want to say?"

Skill: *Ask open-ended questions to draw out people's thoughts and feelings.*

Actions:
- Ask questions that begin with *what, how, describe, explain,* and so forth.
- Ask questions that can't be answered with one word.
- Avoid interrupting people; wait until they have finished.

Skill: *Ask your teams to share status reports.*

Actions:
- At the end of every week, have your group share status reports on important projects and initiatives.
- Have them report what went well, what didn't go well, what they learned, and what specific action steps are planned for the next week.

Skill: *Avoid speaking in a monotone during discussions.*

Action:
- Vary your volume, pitch, and pace to emphasize major points in discussions.

(continued)

Leadership Competency 33:
Communicating Openly and Effectively *(continued)*

Skill: *Be aware of cultural/social differences and business norms.*

Actions:
- When dealing with foreign associates, be aware of cultural differences in social and business norms, and learn how to modify your behavior when necessary.
- Ask someone familiar with a particular country's cultural norms and communication habits which pitfalls you need to avoid.

Skill: *Be willing to discuss the pros and cons of different viewpoints.*

Actions:
- Discussion should begin by accurately acknowledging the opposing points of view.
- Ask a colleague to assess your level of defensiveness regarding your own point of view.
- Manage different perspectives by getting the other point of view, giving your own point of view, and merging images.

Skill: *Check the clarity of your communications.*

Actions:
- Ask others to summarize what you've said and what they think you mean.
- Build your vocabulary: Deliberately use a new word every day.

Skill: *Check your listen-talk ratio.*

Action:
- If you want to be listening, observe the amount of time you are talking. It should be very little! Learn to catch yourself when you are talking (but should be listening).

Skill: *Concentrate on getting your message across.*

Actions:
- If you are nervous, concentrate on getting your message across—not on your ability as a speaker.
- Communicate the "why" behind the "what."

Skill: *Analyze your audience and what they already know.*

Action:
- Consider your audience. What do they know already? What do you want them to do?

Skill: *Design staff meetings that foster more involvement.*

Actions:
- Design your staff meetings so that you are not the sole source of information.
- Ask other people to give updates and share relevant information.
- Evaluate your staff meeting in terms of how much time was spent in "information giving," how much in "information getting," and how much in problem solving or brainstorming.

(continued)

Leadership Competency 33:
Communicating Openly and Effectively (continued)

Skill: *Develop a stakeholder analysis prior to presenting a new idea or plan.*

Actions: • Before presenting a new idea or action plan, list the people whose support you will need.
              • Attempt to discover where each person stands in relation to your proposal— pro, con, or neutral—and formulate a plan to handle each.

Skill: *Develop approaches for informal communication.*

Action: • For the purpose of informal communication, hold monthly breakfast meetings that have no agenda.

Skill: *Deliver concise messages.*

Actions: • Distill your message down to key points.
              • Only include supporting material relevant to those points.

Skill: *Don't ignore or downplay negative issues.*

Actions: • Report on the situation as accurately as possible.
              • Don't punish people who give you negative news.

Skill: *Use multiple forms of communication.*

Actions: • Don't rely only on written communication to inform people; you can't be sure that they will read it.
              • When you do send written messages, edit and proofread your correspondence.

Skill: *Eliminate technical jargon in documents for certain audiences.*

Actions: • Circle all technical jargon in any document meant for a non-technical audience.
              • Then eliminate it or include a glossary.

Skill: *Give your undivided attention to someone you are talking with.*

Action: • Reschedule a conversation if you cannot give the other person your undivided attention.

Skill: *Establish an intranet site to communicate key initiatives, projects, and important topics.*

Actions: • Establish a site on your intranet where people can find current information on strategic initiatives, projects, new clients, and other important topics.
              • Alternatively, establish an e-room (for example, Groove) as an electronic workspace that will enable collaboration.

(continued)

Leadership Competency 33:
Communicating Openly and Effectively *(continued)*

Skill: *Focus on understanding a speaker's meaning.*

Actions:
- Focus on understanding the speaker's meaning, instead of preparing your response.
- Listen to the entire statement.
- Let the speaker finish the thought, instead of forming your response in your head before she or he finishes.
- Summarize the thought in your head and/or verbally summarize the statement before you share your perspective.

Skill: *Hold periodic update meetings to make sure that things are on track.*

Actions:
- Make sure meetings have a clear purpose and agenda.
- Inform participants in advance as to which objectives or projects you are going to be reviewing.

Skill: *Identify your biggest obstacle to listening.*

Action:
- List three things you can do to overcome your listening obstacles. Some of the most common obstacles include: distracting thoughts and emotions, lack of attention, forming your own response in your head, letting judgments about the person block what he or she has to say, and reacting to the beginning statement without hearing the whole message.

Skill: *In international meetings, communicate clearly and completely.*

Actions:
- Check the accuracy of your assumptions.
- Slow the speed of your communication to allow others to process differences in accents, terminology, and ideas.
- Provide extra time for questions, clarifications, and reactions.
- Know the main points you want and need to make. As a rule of thumb, don't present more than three to five main points.

Skill: *Use visual aids to complement your presentation.*

Actions:
- Keep in mind that visual aids should complement your presentation, not act as a substitute for it.
- Don't simply recite your overheads or slides.

Skill: *Learn to recognize when others are resisting your agenda.*

Action:
- Observe verbal and nonverbal behaviors. Signs of possible verbal resistance: constant interruptions or criticisms. Signs of possible non-verbal resistance: not looking at you, facing away from you, rolling eyes, or working on a laptop or personal electronic device when you are talking.

(continued)

Leadership Competency 33:
Communicating Openly and Effectively *(continued)*

Skill: *Pause before answering tough questions.*

Action: • Don't say the first thought that comes into your mind.

Skill: *Pay attention to the feelings being communicated.*

Action: • Pay attention to the feelings being communicated, as well as volume, pace, and tone. They convey critical information, such as importance, sense of urgency, desperation, hope, etc.

Skill: *Position your message in a way that appeals to the audience's needs.*

Actions: • Think about your audience's needs, concerns, and perspectives.
               • Consider how people are likely to react to your message. Whenever possible, position your message in a way that appeals to their needs and avoids strong negative reaction.

Skill: *Prepare the "conceptual" framework of your presentation.*

Action: • Make sure that you thoroughly prepare the "conceptual" framework of your presentation—the purpose of your presentation, the main ideas, etc.

Skill: *Pre-sell your agenda to key players.*

Action: • When faced with possible resistance, consider pre-selling your agenda to a couple of key players.

Skill: *Develop patience.*

Actions: • Realize that true communication takes time.
               • When it is critical for your audience to hear and accept what you have to say, bombard them with multiple messages from multiple sources.

Skill: *Respond non-defensively when people express contrary viewpoints.*

Action: • Ask yourself how much of the time you start your replies with "Yeah, but," or "But I." Forcing yourself to clarify the contrary point by starting out your response with "So you are saying" helps reduce defensiveness.

Skill: *Restate your position to ensure that others understand your perspective.*

Actions: • Don't back down quickly when challenged. Instead, demonstrate your understanding of the challenge.
               • Then, restate your position clearly so that you are sure others can understand your perspective.

(continued)

Leadership Competency 33:
Communicating Openly and Effectively *(concluded)*

Skill: *Seek feedback on your presentation style and delivery.*

Actions:
- Seek feedback on your gestures, grammar, vocal expressiveness, general delivery style, and visual aids after you give a presentation.
- Videotape your presentation and review it critically with an experienced presenter or professional speech coach.
- Seek immediate and specific feedback about a report you have written or presented.

Skill: *Summarize key points on the first page of every report.*

Action:
- When you write a report, summarize your key points and conclusions on the first page.

Skill: *Talk to others about communication breakdowns.*

Actions:
- Talk with peers or people in other departments about any breakdown in communication.
- Devise ways to avoid them. You know there is a breakdown when people have entirely different interpretations of messages that were sent; when there is a great deal of arguing about different points of view; or when people suddenly quit talking.

Skill: *Train employees in how to use the organization's communication technology.*

Action:
- Train telecommuters and in-house personnel on how to use communication technology so that everyone will be able to use the systems efficiently.

Skill: *Use appropriate gestures to animate your discussions.*

Action:
- Ask a peer or a presentation coach to give you feedback on whether your gestures add to your communication effectiveness or distract from it.

Skill: *Use the speakerphone option for conference calls only.*

Action:
- Many people dislike the public nature of the speakerphone option and assume that you are not giving them your full attention. It also inhibits them from bringing up sensitive issues or concerns.

Leadership Competency 34:
Influencing

Skill: *Anticipate the concerns of your audience so that you are prepared.*

Actions: • Listen to your presentation from your audience's perspective.
                • Anticipate their questions, comments, and concerns.
                • Be prepared to answer them from your perspective and from theirs.

Skill: *Solicit feedback about the impact of your activities on others.*

Actions: • Actively solicit information regarding how your activities and projects are impacting others (positively and negatively).
                • Ask others what you should stop, start, and continue.

Skill: *Solicit feedback about your written documents/presentations.*

Actions: • Solicit honest feedback from a trusted peer about your written document and/or presentation before it is submitted.
                • Look for clarity in your message. Measure it by the extent to which the reader can accurately paraphrase the meaning and intent of what you've written.

Skill: *Build trust and rapport.*

Actions: • Do what you say you are going to do.
                • Deliver on your work. More than anything else, honesty is the most critical component in establishing an environment of trust and credibility.
                • Assess the other person's motivation and learning style before trying to sell your idea.

Skill: *Set a positive tone.*

Actions: • Inquire about the other person's thoughts on meeting a challenge, solving a problem, or making a decision.
                • Propose possible solutions, instead of trying to impose.
                • Ask yourself, "How often do I impose vs. propose?"

Skill: *Create positive partnerships.*

Actions: • Work collaboratively with others to get work done and to influence how it gets done.
                • Create conditions where all parties give and receive feedback openly.
                • Assess the other person's commitment and ability to work collaboratively.

Leadership Competency 35: Interviewing

Skill: *Prepare for the interview.*

Actions:
- Learn as much about the individual as you can before the interview.
- Review their résumé and job history.
- Inquire about their interests and hobbies.

Skill: *Attend to the person you are interviewing.*

Actions:
- Make the person feel comfortable and safe.
- Try to create an environmental context that is welcoming. For example, sit in a chair of equal height across from the interviewee. Square your shoulders to them, lean slightly forward, and maintain eye contact.
- Adjust your position to make the individual feel comfortable.

Skill: *Observe the individual's non-verbal behavior.*

Actions:
- Take into account their appearance and behavior.
- Make inferences about feelings, values, relationship, and energy level, based on facts.
- Ask yourself, "Am I aware of the inferences I am making? Are they grounded in fact? Am I suspending judgment and staying open to new information?"

Skill: *Listen to what the interviewee is saying.*

Actions:
- Encourage the interviewee to speak, and let them finish their thoughts without interruptions.
- Resist distractions, suspend judgment, recall content, reflect on pace, volume, and tone, filter out key words, and paraphrase what the person is saying to check your understanding.

Skill: *Respond to the content and meaning of what the interviewee is saying.*

Actions:
- Reflect on the key words and feelings expressed.
- Summarize in your head the feelings and meaning.
- Respond concisely in a way that will demonstrate your understanding.
- Ask yourself, "Am I hearing accurately and completely what the person is expressing verbally and non-verbally?"

(continued)

Leadership Competency 35:
Interviewing *(concluded)*

Skill:	*Ask behaviorally based questions.*
Actions:	• Study the competencies required for success in the job you are hiring for.
	• Identify for yourself the behaviors you would see if the person possessed those competencies.
	• Ask questions that will give you information about how well the person has performed those behaviors in the past.

Skill:	*Give your point of view.*
Actions:	• Share your point of view when it is needed or appropriate.
	• Summarize in your head what you want to say, and then say it as clearly as possible without using inflammatory words or tones.
	• Listen to the person's reaction and response and demonstrate understanding of that feedback.

Leadership Competency 36:
Listening

Skill: *Suspend judgment.*

Actions:
- Stay open to new information.
- Ask yourself, "Am I aware of biases I hold concerning this person?" If you identify judgments you are making, try to suspend them.

Skill: *Resist distractions.*

Actions:
- Look for ways to reduce environmental noise.
- Don't accept phone calls or interruptions during a meeting.
- Be aware of how often you are distracted and what distracting behaviors you are doing (e.g., tapping your foot or playing with a paper clip).
- Observe yourself, and try to re-focus when your mind wanders.
- Be careful not to get so caught up in the story line that you quit listening.

Skill: *Recall content.*

Actions:
- Let the person complete his or her thoughts.
- Re-play in your mind what the person said.
- Ask yourself, "Did I hear it all?"

Skill: *Listen for key words.*

Actions:
- As you listen, filter out key words that suggest feelings or values.
- Look for words or phrases that have real meaning to the person.

Skill: *Reflect on volume, tone, and pace.*

Actions:
- Listen not only for what was said, but how it was said.
- Ask yourself, "What do the volume, tone, and pace tell me about this person?"

Skill: *Paraphrase content.*

Actions:
- Reflect on the key words and feelings expressed.
- Summarize in your head the feelings and meaning.
- Respond in a concise way that demonstrates your understanding.
- Ask yourself, "Am I hearing accurately and completely what the person is expressing verbally and non-verbally?"

Leadership Competency 37:
Consulting Effectively

Skill: *Seek out role models who demonstrate good coaching and consulting skills.*

Action: • Watch them in action, or work with them on a project to learn their
               techniques.

Skill: *Facilitate a strategic-planning session.*

Actions: • Work with an executive to conduct an off-site retreat.
               • Write the purpose and agenda for the meeting.
               • Help the team develop or refine its vision, values, mission, goals,
                 and objectives.

Skill: *Conduct a culture audit.*

Actions: • Create a survey instrument by listing the core values and desired norms for
                 the work environment.
               • Ask for perceptions on the strength, importance, and direction of the stated
                 norms and values.
               • Analyze the results and communicate them to the team.

Skill: *Lead a team-building activity off-site.*

Actions: • Assess the stage of development, the level of effectiveness, and the degree
                 of virtuality of the team.
               • Hold a two-day off-site session to clarify direction and to deal with major
                 challenges.
               • Facilitate a feedback session in which each member hears about the
                 behaviors that other team members wish he or she would start, stop,
                 or continue.
               • Identify communication and decision-making issues, and explore ways to
                 improve.

Skill: *Consult with an executive on a major issue.*

Actions: • Identify a critical issue a business leader is trying to solve (e.g., how to
                 reduce the time it takes to design and produce new products).
               • Work closely with the executive to define the problem, identify the root
                 causes, and generate possible solutions.
               • Investigate the strengths and weaknesses in the organization that could
                 impact successful implementation.
               • Partner with the executive to ensure that the solution is implemented and
                 that you achieve the desired results.

(continued)

Leadership Competency 37:
Consulting Effectively *(concluded)*

Skill: *Conduct leadership reviews.*

Actions:
- Identify bench strength for critical jobs in the organization.
- For each person who is listed in the succession plan, evaluate their performance, potential, and readiness to move into another job.
- Ask yourself, "Do I have a balanced perspective on strengths and weaknesses, as well as behavior and results?"

Skill: *Develop a contract for services.*

Actions:
- Make explicit agreements on expectations for the consultant and the client.
- Agree on the results you are trying to achieve, the method for delivering the results, and how you are going to work together.
- Assess the situation in terms of the scope, approach, time frames and urgency, roles, and resource requirements.
- Explore alternative ways to deliver the project.

Skill: *Engage in productive dialogue.*

Actions:
- Get the client's perspective.
- Give your own point of view and perspective.
- Merge images and generate better ideas.
- Develop the capability to engage clients through inquiry, advocacy, mental modeling, and generative thinking.

Skill: *Position yourself with clients.*

Actions:
- Create the perception of serving as a value-added partner for business solutions.
- Describe a range of possible outcomes from a given intervention.
- Determine the gap between the current state and the desired state.
- Discover as much as you can about your client's business.
- Demonstrate that you can add value to business challenges at high levels.

Skill: *Develop core skills in consulting.*

Action:
- Assess yourself on the core skills of consulting: goal setting, data gathering and analysis, problem solving, planning and project management, and evaluation. If you have gaps, take courses to improve your core skills.

Leadership Competency 38:
Giving and Receiving Feedback

Skill: *Seek feedback from people you trust.*

Actions:
- Ask a respected colleague or manager with whom you regularly interact in one-to-one and group situations to give you feedback from time to time.
- Ask for the person's impressions of your style and impact in a variety of situations.
- Seek feedback about behaviors you are trying to change.

Skill: *Cultivate strong interpersonal skills.*

Actions:
- Learn how to listen, observe, attend, and respond effectively.
- When you are in a difficult situation, make sure you listen first and demonstrate understanding before offering your perspective.
- Before offering feedback or giving advice, make sure you fully understand the situation at hand and the other person's feelings and experience.

Skill: *Establish a safe environment for giving and receiving feedback.*

Actions:
- Schedule a feedback session at the right time to ensure a positive experience, and allow enough time so that no one feels rushed.
- Regularly check in with people to foster open communication and a trusting environment.
- Discuss sensitive information privately and in person. Communicate face-to-face when you need to discuss something important.

Skill: *Know the characteristics of high-impact feedback.*

Actions:
- View feedback as a process of discovery rather than a declaration.
- Make sure you present factual and nonjudgmental information, rather than make "positive" or "negative" remarks.
- Provide feedback that gives people information about where they stand relative to their goals.
- Phrase your feedback in terms of behaviors, potential impact, and likely consequences.

Skill: *Ask people what kind of feedback and support they would like from you.*

Actions:
- Identify supports that are behavioral, actionable, and observable.
- Restate the types of feedback and support that people want from you so that you will be sure your images are similar.

Skill: *Be alert to articles and development tips that could be of help to others.*

Action:
- When you find important developmental information online, cut and paste the address into your browser, and e-mail the item to others who can also benefit.

(continued)

Leadership Competency 38:
Giving and Receiving Feedback *(continued)*

Skill: *Conduct an off-site workshop with the team on how to improve team performance.*

Actions:
- Have the group make three lists: A list of the behaviors to stop, a list of behaviors to start, and a list of behaviors to continue.
- Identify the two most important items from each list, and gain group commitment to adhere to the "new norms."

Skill: *Discuss career goals with your employees.*

Actions:
- Meet individually with your employees to discuss their career goals and identify the skills they need to achieve those goals.
- Have each employee list his/her top three professional goals or values.
- Make the connection between what they value most and what they may need to learn to achieve those goals.
- Discuss positions where they can achieve those goals.
- Outline a career plan based on achieving those goals.
- Set reasonable time frames.

Skill: *Connect people with role models and mentors.*

Actions:
- Connect people with role models and mentors who possess the skills they are trying to develop.
- Be sure to orient each potential mentor with a personalized goal statement regarding the person they are being asked to mentor.
- Clearly state why and how you and your employees will benefit from a successful mentorship.

Skill: *Develop a network of cross-functional contacts for advice.*

Actions:
- Develop a network of cross-functional contacts to tap into during project execution.
- List all of the colleagues in your network. Assign each one a weight ranging from 1 to 5, with 5 representing the closest possible relationship.
- List each person's specific expertise.
- Reference this list as your learning source when seeking specific advice.

Skill: *Develop a team-feedback approach.*

Actions:
- Develop a team approach and system for providing constructive feedback to one another.
- Let each person critique themselves first. Then let the rest of the team take a turn before you do.
- Be aware of how well each person can identify "excellent" performance and how interpersonally skilled each is at giving feedback.
- Give feedback to the entire group along both dimensions.

(continued)

Leadership Competency 38:
Giving and Receiving Feedback *(continued)*

Skill: *Develop performance management systems that support business strategies.*

Actions: • Develop performance management systems that support the business strategies and goals (e.g., analyze current systems and make recommendations).
  • Identify your organization's business objectives first.
  • Then, identify each employee's performance objectives in that context. The accomplishment of employee objectives should result in organizational success. The gaps in performance either become skill development needs for the employees or support development needs for your organization.

Skill: *Develop succession planning processes and tools.*

Actions: • Rate each employee according to competence, commitment, and cultural fit.
  • Rate each position the same way.
  • Identify employees who show potential for future positions.
  • Identify the gap between the employee's present level of functioning and what is needed to move up.
  • Develop a performance plan for those employees you want to involve in succession planning.

Skill: *Emphasize development in performance management practices.*

Action: • Make sure that each employee is working on at least one measurable learning goal at all times. The learning goal should be related to critical competency requirements.

Skill: *Encourage employees to expand their comfort zone.*

Actions: • Ask employees to identify one activity that they do not perform well.
  • Have them identify an in-house mentor or "expert" to consult.
  • Then have them develop a specific goal for activity improvement (with a timeline attached).
  • Monitor their progress regularly.
  • Note any change in performance, and reinforce their positive efforts.

Skill: *Encourage people to focus their development efforts.*

Actions: • Encourage people to focus their development efforts on areas where they can achieve the greatest leverage.
  • Make sure that their development plan matches their values, their organization's objectives, their job performance objectives, and their immediate interests.

(continued)

Leadership Competency 38:
Giving and Receiving Feedback *(continued)*

Skill: *Encourage people to treat feedback as a hypothesis to be tested.*

Actions:
- Teach people to accurately restate the feedback they have been given before agreeing or disagreeing as an exercise in listening and personalizing.
- Make sure they understand that good feedback is not imposed; it is suggested behavior that the recipient should test.

Skill: *Establish clear standards and expectations with your team.*

Actions:
- Quantify your goals (e.g., "number of" or "percentage of").
- Create a 5-point scale, with level 3 being the minimally accepted level of accomplishment.
- Make sure that your level-3 response is fair but not too easily achievable.

Skill: *Establish processes that promote learning from each other.*

Actions:
- Establish processes that promote learning from each other, both within and across departments.
- Identify the knowledge and skill needs of your team.
- Identify the best learning sources within and between teams and organizations.
- Create explicit links to those knowledge sources.
- Create expectations for learners and the learning sources.

Skill: *Find ways to enrich the jobs of your employees.*

Actions:
- Find ways to enrich the jobs of your employees by increasing their authority or span of control.
- Allow each team member to identify a new responsibility to manage in a particular project and monitor their progress.

Skill: *Focus your feedback on people's behavior.*

Actions:
- Be more descriptive and less evaluative in your feedback.
- Begin by identifying the positive behaviors.
- Then identify up to three negative behaviors, and suggest ways to change them.
- Always ask the person to paraphrase your feedback so that you are sure they understand.
- Then ask for their reaction so that you know how the feedback was received.

Skill: *Use the buddy system for performance feedback.*

Actions:
- Ask for feedback that is specific, behavioral, and measurable, and ask for actionable prescriptions for improved performance.
- Restate what you've been told to make sure you understand.
- Do the same for your feedback partner.

(continued)

Leadership Competency 38:
Giving and Receiving Feedback *(continued)*

Skill: *Give your employees specific, relevant feedback.*

Actions:
- Make sure people get specific, relevant information about their performance.
- Begin by stating the positive attributes in their performance.
- Then identify one or two behaviors that need to be eliminated or improved. Give a behavioral example of the suggested improvement.

Skill: *Help employees clarify their personal goals and values.*

Actions:
- Ask employees to describe their perfect job.
- Sort out the job attributes by physical, emotional, and intellectual dimensions.
- Have the employees rate the attributes by importance.
- Ask the employees to rate their current and needed level of functioning.
- Explore ways to develop competencies to meet the needed level.

Skill: *Help people reflect and learn from their successes and failures.*

Actions:
- Set time aside after a major project success or failure to do a postmortem.
- List what went well and what didn't. List the major learnings and the recommended actions for the next project.
- Reserve judgment. Most people already know most of the criticism that is directed toward them.

Skill: *Provide feedback that is contextual and behavioral.*

Actions:
- Practice taking notes so that you can provide constructive feedback that is meaningful to the person.
- Be sure to note your overall impressions of performance, as well as the specifics.
- Also, be sure to note positive and negative attributes.
- Be prepared to state corrective actions behaviorally.

Skill: *Maintain a development file on each of your employees.*

Actions:
- Keep track of their goals, abilities, perceptions of others, successes and failures, and record how you have agreed to help.
- Rate each person as either a Leader, Contributor, Participant, Observer, or Detractor for each project.

(continued)

Leadership Competency 38:
Giving and Receiving Feedback *(continued)*

Skill: *Give feedback that is specific and behavioral.*

Actions:
- When an individual achieves a goal or completes work, make sure to give positive feedback to reinforce the behavior.
- Involve the individual by asking them what they are most proud of concerning their latest accomplishment. This will give you insight into what they value most.

Skill: *Publicly recognize and reward people who develop themselves and others.*

Actions:
- Create a quarterly award to be presented to individuals who demonstrate personal or team development.
- Present the reward in a quarterly meeting or forum.

Skill: *Recognize development efforts, not just results.*

Actions:
- Use the principle of "successive approximation."
- Identify and reinforce the positive behaviors, independent of the results.
- Identify the areas needed for improvement, and state them behaviorally.
- Be specific about next steps.
- Reinforce the overall effort positively to keep the employee energized.

Skill: *Remember that people master tasks in small steps.*

Actions:
- Help your employees become competent by gradually increasing their responsibilities.
- Build success into their development plans in order to increase confidence and motivation.

Skill: *Seek out opportunities to mentor others.*

Actions:
- Find people who have a reputation for success.
- Ask them to mentor you.
- Find out the methods and processes they employ.
- Try to replicate their process.

Skill: *Teach employees how to get feedback for themselves.*

Actions:
- Tell employees that asking for help is culturally appropriate if and when it makes a difference in accomplishing an organization's goals.
- Make sure that you intend to learn from the support that you receive, in order to minimize the need for future support in a similar situation.

(continued)

Leadership Competency 38:
Giving and Receiving Feedback *(concluded)*

Skill: *Use 360° assessments as a way to provide developmental advice to your team.*

Actions: • Decide how confidential the 360° results are.
               • Hold a feedback session to help people understand the results.
               • Provide expert coaching (i.e., an outside consultant) for each individual, as appropriate.

Skill: *Work on an assignment with a key business leader.*

Actions: • Get involved in an assignment or extended project that requires you to work with a key business leader(s) to analyze and improve business structures and processes and balance management and constituency interests.
               • Ask for feedback on your own performance.

Leadership Competency 39: Being Honest

Skill: *Meet your commitments.*

Actions:
- Do what you say you are going to do.
- Deliver on your work.
- More than anything else, honesty is the most critical part of establishing an environment of trust and credibility.

Skill: *Give genuine feedback.*

Action:
- When someone asks for feedback, give an honest response. You don't need to say everything you think or feel, but make sure what you do say is genuine.

Skill: *Answer accurately.*

Actions:
- Give honest answers to the questions you are asked.
- Remember, it is more important to be accurate than to be clever.

Skill: *Share your perspective.*

Actions:
- Contribute your point of view in dialogue that matters to you and to the company.
- Decide how much you want to disclose about yourself and how you are thinking and feeling.
- When you share your perspective, make sure it is clear and concise and that it contains no "red flags" or inflammatory language.
- Remember, you can deliver a hard message in a respectful way.

Skill: *Tell the truth.*

Actions:
- Say what you think and say what you mean.
- Strive to be as direct as you can.
- If there is a problem, bring it up so that it can be addressed.

Skill: *Seek congruence between values and behaviors.*

Actions:
- Write down the 10 values that are most important to you.
- Ask yourself, "How aligned are my behaviors with my values?"
- Identify the values you are violating with your behaviors.
- Seek to close the gaps.

Skill: *Admit your mistakes.*

Actions:
- Take responsibility for your role in a problem.
- Don't try to hide your role or deny that you made a mistake.
- Ask yourself, "How often do I get defensive about my mistakes, instead of taking responsibility for them?"

(continued)

Leadership Competency 39:
Being Honest *(concluded)*

Skill: *Refuse to lie, steal, or cheat.*

Actions: • If you are asked to fudge the truth or engage in unethical practices, refuse.
                • Remember, you have two responsibilities here: not to collude, and to expose dishonest behavior when you are aware of it to protect the company.

Leadership Competency 40: Mentoring

Skill: *Ask a knowledgeable person to be your mentor.*

Action:
- Ask a knowledgeable and well-connected person in your part of the organization to act as your mentor.

Skill: *Make connections with potential role models and mentors.*

Actions:
- Clarify your strengths and developmental needs. What skills, knowledge, or tools do you need, and who might be willing and able to provide them?
- Make a list of all possible contacts, and take steps to make a connection with them in order to stretch and grow.

Skill: *Orchestrate learning opportunities.*

Actions:
- Find ways to give your employees assignments that provide important developmental opportunities such as representing you at a meeting, leading a cross-functional task force, introducing them to a senior manager, or becoming a mentor to a new or inexperienced employee.
- Ask yourself how you can help employees network with the right people and gain access to resources, new skills, and important learning opportunities.

Skill: *Create a work environment that promotes development.*

Actions:
- Cultivate a safe atmosphere by actively promoting experimentation and giving employees permission to make mistakes (as long as they learn from them).
- Openly and enthusiastically recognize people who attempt to go beyond what is expected.
- Demonstrate your own commitment to development by sharing your development objectives and asking for regular feedback.

Leadership Competency 41: Presenting

Skill: *Deliver effective low-risk presentations.*

Action: • Give speeches at community or service organizations, or take classes in which you have to make regular presentations.

Skill: *Project a credible image with polish and poise.*

Actions: • Be aware of your physical presence and the way in which your voice communicates confidence, control, and calm.
              • If you are nervous or anxious about public presentations, find ways to relax and get focused prior to your presentation.
              • Visualize the confidence and poise you want to project, and believe that you can actualize that image of yourself.

Skill: *Handle questions well in highly visible, adversarial situations.*

Actions: • Follow a two-thirds/one-third guideline: Spend two-thirds of your time presenting or speaking, and spend one-third of your time answering questions and having discussion.
              • Be ready for every kind of question, and prepare your responses ahead of time.
              • Make sure you understand the question being posed. Give yourself time to briefly reflect if necessary, and answer as concisely as possible.

Skill: *Lead effective meetings.*

Actions: • Make sure the meeting is actually necessary.
              • Determine what the purpose, agenda, and expected outcomes are for the meeting several days in advance, and communicate this so that participants can come prepared.
              • Keep your meetings moving forward by striking a balance between permissiveness and progress. Is the discussion moving you closer to clarity, decision, or commitment?

Skill: *Deliver clear, well-organized presentations.*

Actions: • Make sure your presentation is meeting the needs of your audience: Go over who will be there, what the goals and expectations of the presentation are, and what outcomes you are striving for.
              • Determine what format you will use to present information.
              • State clearly for the audience the major themes, topics, and goals for the presentation so that you focus their attention on the central ideas.
              • Deliver your content with a well-balanced mix of facts, anecdotes, quotations, and explanations.

(continued)

Leadership Competency 41:
Presenting *(continued)*

Skill: *Engage the audience during presentations.*

Actions:
- If you are unfamiliar with a potential audience, take time to walk around and talk to people before you speak.
- Ask the audience rhetorical or actual questions, which will prompt them to think about your topic.
- Explain the impact your presentation will have on participants. This will give them a reason to actively listen and participate.
- Gauge your audience's reaction as you speak. Are they losing interest? Are they confused or restless?
- Ask yourself how you can refocus your presentation and reach the audience more effectively.

Skill: *Create a clear and specific goal for your presentation.*

Actions:
- Write down the desired outcome for your presentation.
- List the three major points you want to cover.

Skill: *Create impressive presentations.*

Actions:
- Organize your presentation so that it is easy to read and visually pleasing.
- Don't try to put too much information on any one slide.
- Use colors and art to make your presentation more appealing, but don't overuse either one.
- Take a course in PowerPoint® to improve your skills.

Skill: *Analyze the audience to determine their needs and wants.*

Actions:
- Always ask who you are presenting to.
- Inquire about levels of knowledge, skills, and experience.
- Tailor your remarks in a way that respects the experiences of your audience.
- Ask yourself, "Are my remarks above or below what my audience will understand?"

Skill: *Connect to what you are saying.*

Actions:
- Speak genuinely.
- Make sure your remarks are real and meaningful to you.
- Don't try to fake enthusiasm, but don't be afraid to show your passion if you feel it.

Skill: *Develop a compelling presence.*

Actions:
- Attend to your non-verbal behavior.
- Eliminate any fidgeting or nervous gestures.
- Stand tall, and project a feeling of confidence.

(continued)

Leadership Competency 41:
Presenting *(concluded)*

Skill:	*Provide focus and clarity.*
Actions:	• Make your points clearly and concisely.
	• Don't ramble.
	• Stick with your key points, and provide supporting evidence and feeling.

Skill:	*Grab your audience's attention.*
Actions:	• Take time to understand the perspective, needs, and interests of your audience.
	• Make a statement at the beginning of your presentation that indicates you did your research. If you have a dramatic fact or story that is related to your presentation, use it early.

Skill:	*Use simple techniques.*
Actions:	• Never turn your back to the audience.
	• Don't rush through your presentation or try to cram too much information into too short a time.
	• Establish eye contact with members of your audience.
	• If you are using a projector, use a laser pointer to refer to some critical points.

Skill:	*Handle challenging comments and questions.*
Actions:	• Clarify questions before you answer them.
	• Make sure you understand the question or comment that is raised before you give a response.
	• Stay calm, and give a rational response.
	• Ask yourself, "Do I have sufficient evidence to support my assertions?"

Leadership Competency 42: Practicing Business Etiquette

Skill:	*Be courteous and thoughtful.*
Actions:	• Be polite and mindful of other people's comfort level and circumstances. • Ask yourself, "Do I think about ways to make people feel welcome and respected?"

Skill:	*Talk and visit with people.*
Actions:	• Ask people questions about their interests. • Listen to their stories. • Ask yourself, "Am I doing more listening than talking?" • Stay focused on the person you are talking with.

Skill:	*Impressing the boss isn't enough.*
Actions:	• Be sure to attend to people at all levels of the organization—not just to superiors. • Ask yourself, "How much time do I spend talking with my peers and the people who report to me?" • Work as hard at showing your best side to peers and employees as you do to your boss.

Skill:	*Never surprise your boss.*
Actions:	• Keep your boss informed of changes and developments. If there is bad news, make sure you keep your boss apprised. • Ask yourself every week, "Are there issues I need to bring up with my boss?"

Skill:	*Don't pretend to be fluent.*
Action:	• Be honest about your language skills. It is better to understate your fluency than to overstate it.

Skill:	*Be considerate of time zones.*
Actions:	• When you set up a meeting or schedule a phone call, think about what time it will be for every person who is involved. • Ask yourself, "What percentage of calls or meetings am I scheduling at times that are convenient for me vs. what is convenient for other people?"

(continued)

Leadership Competency 42:
Practicing Business Etiquette *(concluded)*

Skill: *Return phone calls.*

Actions: • Let people know what your standards are for returning phone calls.
               • Whenever possible, return calls within 24 hours.
               • Consider setting aside time in your day that is solely devoted to taking and making phone calls.

Skill: *Avoid interruptions.*

Actions: • When you are meeting with people or you are on the phone with someone, try to stay focused during the entire time.
               • Don't take phone calls when you are in a meeting, and don't abandon one conversation if someone appears whom you would rather talk to.
               • Always consider the impact of your behavior on the other person.

Skill: *Make e-mail subject lines specific.*

Actions: • When writing an e-mail message, use the subject line to let the reader know what the message is about.
               • Ask yourself, "Will this subject line give my readers a good sense of what this e-mail will be about?"

Skill: *Research table manners.*

Actions: • When you are planning a trip to another country, inquire in advance about acceptable and non-acceptable behavior and table manners.
               • Be sensitive to the customs of the country you are working in.

Skill: *Give credit to contributors.*

Actions: • Make sure you recognize people for their contributions.
               • Ask yourself, "Am I distributing credit fairly, or am I taking too much credit for myself?"

Leadership Competency 43:
Business Writing

Skill: *Develop a plan for your writing.*

Actions:
- Organize your thoughts and develop an outline.
- Think in advance how long the writing should be.
- Take into consideration where the reader is coming from.
- Create a timeline for the writing, and carve out enough time in your schedule to do it justice.

Skill: *Create coherent paragraphs that clearly communicate the point.*

Actions:
- Identify the main point for each paragraph.
- State the main point in the opening sentence of the paragraph.
- Develop three to four supporting statements to substantiate your point.
- Ask yourself, "Is this paragraph as concise as it can be, and is the point clear?"

Skill: *Recognize good sentence structure.*

Actions:
- Make sure your sentences are clear.
- Decide on the subject and action verb for each sentence.
- Check to see that tenses are consistent and that your action verbs are appropriate for the noun.

Skill: *Create concise, memorable sentences.*

Actions:
- Try to find the best adjectives to support your nouns and the best adverbs to describe your verbs.
- Be more concerned with accuracy than cleverness, but express yourself as forcefully as the situation merits.
- Remember, shorter is usually better.

Skill: *Delete unnecessary words and phrases.*

Actions:
- Avoid jargon and slang.
- After you have written your paragraphs, go back and review them to see if you can get rid of words and phrases that are redundant or that clutter the message.
- Consider the lesson in Pascal's words: "I have made this letter longer because I lack the time to make it shorter."

Skill: *Transform reports from vague to specific.*

Actions:
- Look for ways to make your paragraphs and sentences more concrete.
- Give as many details as necessary for your reader to understand your point.
- Ask yourself, "Who is going to be reading this report?"
- Make it as specific as you need to satisfy the reader's requirements, learning style, and preference. Remember: Some people only like to have the big picture. Others can't get enough details.

Leadership Competency 44:
Building Cognitive Skills

Skill: *Learn how to learn.*

Actions: • Use a simple formula to learn: explore, understand, and act.
               • Start out by keeping your mind open and considering a wide range of options.
               • After you exhaust your tolerance for input, try to reach an understanding of the major issues.
               • Don't forget: One of the best ways to learn is to take action and then process the results.

Skill: *Learn how to think.*

Actions: • Assess whether you are an independent or an *inter*dependent thinker.
               • Share your ideas with other people and get feedback.
               • Analyze problems three-dimensionally by capturing the components, functions, and processes of any given problem.
               • Represent your thinking in non-linear form. Read books on lateral thinking and systems thinking.

Skill: *Learn how to reason.*

Actions: • Describe a situation as completely as possible.
               • Identify the ways that problems are manifested in a given situation.
               • Seek out the root causes of a problem by organizing the data into categories: people, process, and technology or culture.
               • Brainstorm ways to address the root causes and solve the problem.

Skill: *Learn how to memorize.*

Actions: • Practice memorizing lists of names.
               • When you are in a meeting with new people, learn each person's name and memorize it as soon as you can.
               • Go to the Internet and explore resources for improving your ability to memorize.

Skill: *Learn how to solve.*

Actions: • Identify a problem that needs to be solved.
               • Frame the problem in a concise and accurate way.
               • Brainstorm possible root causes for the problem.
               • Narrow the list of possible causes to those that account for 80 percent of the variance.
               • Brainstorm possible solutions to the problem.
               • Choose the best solution, based on well-defined criteria for success.

(continued)

Leadership Competency 44:
Building Cognitive Skills *(concluded)*

Skill: *Learn how to organize.*

Actions:
- Make a list of things to do each day.
- Establish a course of action for yourself and others to accomplish specific results.
- Prepare short- and long-term goals.
- Check out the Internet for tips on organizing (e.g., when recording your voice mail greeting, ask that the caller leave a message indicating the best time to return the call).
- Ask yourself, "Is what I am doing urgent and important?" If not, move on to something else.

Section 2—Building Team Capabilities

Leadership Competency 45	Building High Performance Teams
Leadership Competency 46	Building Cross-Functional Teams
Leadership Competency 47	Building Self-Directed Teams
Leadership Competency 48	Building Commitment
Leadership Competency 49	Building Consensus

Leadership Competency 45: Building High Performance Teams

Skill: *Lead a large project involving multiple teams.*

Actions:
- Lead a large project that requires you to form multiple but integrated teams; clarify and facilitate the performance of responsibilities with team leaders; and negotiate and coordinate significant resources.
- Lead an organization that supports one or more businesses involved with such activities as establishing effective communications with business teams, developing methodologies and procedures, and creating a positive internal and external team environment.
- When leading a large project that involves other functions, set up regular review meetings to ensure that things are on track.

Skill: *Assess team effectiveness.*

Actions:
- Assess commitment, capability, and culture.
- Determine the strength, importance, and direction of critical standards of team effectiveness.
- Address any gaps between importance and effectiveness.

Skill: *Assess virtuality.*

Actions:
- Identify the virtual characteristics of the team that will need to be taken into account in order for the team to be successful.
- Determine how many locations, time zones, levels, departments, organizations, and cultures are represented on the team.

Skill: *Assess the team's current stage of development.*

Actions:
- Determine which stage of development the team is in: orientation, trust building, goal clarification, decision making, implementation, high performance, or renewal.
- Develop a plan to get to high performance.

(continued)

Leadership Competency 45:
Building High Performance Teams *(continued)*

Skill: *Prioritize major issues and opportunities.*

Actions: • Identify changes and challenges.
                • Identify make-or-break issues.
                • Conduct problem-solving sessions to address top priorities.

Skill: *Develop a common purpose and a set of principles.*

Actions: • Articulate the vision.
                • Define the values.
                • Agree on operating principles and norms.

Skill: *Establish a plan.*

Actions: • Define the mission.
                • Develop goals and objectives.

Skill: *Define roles and responsibilities.*

Actions: • Distribute tasks and accountabilities.
                • Define categories of information that will need to be collected and shared.
                • Describe the key events facing the team.

Skill: *Value differences.*

Actions: • Understand personal profiles through an assessment tool.
                • Understand how differences contribute to team effectiveness.
                • Develop a plan for leveraging differences.

Skill: *Use interpersonal skills.*

Actions: • Listen to each other.
                • Ask questions.
                • Demonstrate understanding.
                • Give your perspective.
                • Manage conflict.

Skill: *Demonstrate leadership.*

Actions: • Lead virtually by creating an electronic workspace.
                • Facilitate teamwork.
                • Manage team communication.

(continued)

Leadership Competency 45:
Building High Performance Teams *(concluded)*

Skill: *Address virtual challenges.*

Action:
- Discuss challenges and strategies related to participation, problem solving, rewards and recognition, learning, communication, and trust.

Skill: *Create an aspirational statement.*

Actions:
- Develop a vision that challenges the entire organization.
- Describe the ideal end state for the organization.
- Ask yourself, "What are the headlines I would like to read five years from now that would describe the state of our business?"

Skill: *Create an inspirational statement.*

Actions:
- Develop a vision that reflects the values of as many of your employees as possible and that motivates them to perform at their highest levels.
- Ask yourself, "Would I want to have my picture taken next to this vision statement?"

Skill: *Describe the ideal end state.*

Actions:
- Expand measures of success.
- Write down what team success would look like to you at the end of five years.
- Ask yourself, "How will I know if we have been successful?"

Leadership Competency 46: Building Cross-Functional Teams

Skill: *Define success criteria.*

Actions: • Clarify what success looks like after a specific period of time during
                   which a cross-functional team works together.
               • Determine the desired outcome, and scale it from 1 to 5
                   (1 = *totally unacceptable,* 3 = *acceptable,* and 5 = *ideal*).
               • Ask yourself, "How will I know if this team has been successful?"
               • Identify why the team has been formed: to solve a problem that impacts
                   multiple parts of the organization, to improve a work process that crosses
                   organizational lines, or to accomplish tasks that require a breadth and depth
                   of knowledge, skills, and experience.

Skill: *Select the right members.*

Actions: • Select team members who have the optimal mix of skills and experience for
                   the outcomes you are trying to achieve.
               • Identify the roles and responsibilities of team members.
               • Provide team members with access to training in teamwork skills such as
                   communicating, problem solving, action planning, and facilitating.

Skill: *Specify objectives and deliverables.*

Actions: • Reach team agreement on the objectives and deliverables.
               • Set specific, measurable objectives, and make them time-bound.
               • Clarify the deliverables and milestones.
               • Discuss the people, process, technology, culture, and knowledge capabilities
                   you will need if you are to successfully achieve each objective.

Skill: *Get stakeholder buy-in for criteria, objectives, and deliverables.*

Actions: • List all the stakeholders for this cross-functional team.
               • Share with them the desired outcomes, specific objectives and deliverables,
                   and the resources required to develop your capabilities and achieve your
                   objectives in the agreed-upon time.
               • Ask yourself, "Do we have buy-in, commitment, and the necessary support
                   from the stakeholders of this team?"

Skill: *Solicit feedback on contributions.*

Actions: • When working on a cross-functional team, seek out feedback from your
                   colleagues on the contributions they are hoping you have made and on
                   the contributions you think you have made.
               • Ask yourself, "Am I clear about my role and responsibilities and how I
                   contribute to this team? And is this a shared view?"

(continued)

Leadership Competency 46:
Building Cross-Functional Teams *(concluded)*

Skill: *Determine the trade-off between functional contribution and cross-functional contribution.*

Actions:
- Working on a cross-functional team sometimes means that you have less time to work on your "regular" functional team.
- Talk with your boss and your peers about how participation on the cross-functional team might affect your "regular" work.
- Be clear about the trade-offs, and communicate them.

Skill: *Evaluate success.*

Actions:
- Review progress against stated objectives and deliverables.
- Ask yourself, "At what level did we achieve the desired outcome?"
- Identify the reasons for your success and/or lack of success.
- Reward the team accordingly.

Leadership Competency 47:
Building Self-Directed Teams

Skill: *Develop a customer focus.*

Actions: • Be clear that all teams exist for an external reason.
               • Make sure the team retains its commitment to add value to the customer.
               • Build teams around process improvement.

Skill: *Align the team around a common vision and mission.*

Actions: • Clarify how the team's mission relates to the organization and business mission.
               • Define the roles of individual members within the team, as well as the team's role in the organization.

Skill: *Develop skills for working together.*

Actions: • Teach team members how to make decisions, plan work, and resolve differences.
               • Encourage interdependence and trust.
               • Develop a sense of "we" so that the team accepts joint responsibility.

Skill: *Empower the team to improve work and achieve results.*

Actions: • Set parameters and direction.
               • Start with a few critical empowerments.
               • Provide an appropriate degree of autonomy and support to the team.

Skill: *Set goals and solve problems.*

Actions: • Strive for continuous improvement in inputs, processing, and outputs.
               • Equip the team with appropriate tools and methodologies, and dedicate the time to learn and use them.
               • Make sure the team understands that continuous improvement is its responsibility.

Skill: *Train managers to support the teams.*

Actions: • Involve management in the transition over to self-directed teams.
               • Teach managers how to guide the team in its transition, development, and empowerment.
               • Help managers understand when to hold on and when to let go.
               • Teach managers how to provide ongoing coaching support.

Leadership Competency 48:
Building Commitment

Skill:	*Win emotional commitment.*
Actions:	• Create a vision statement that is aspirational and inspirational and that taps into the deepest values of employees. • Communicate the vision in a way that inspires employees to mobilize behind it. • Use the following scale to rate how well you have communicated the vision and motivated employees to increase their commitment: 1 = *ignored employees;* 2 = *informed employees;* 3 = *involved employees;* 4 = *incorporated employees;* 5 = *inspired employees.*

Skill:	*Win intellectual commitment.*
Actions:	• Create a mission statement that accurately describes the nature and purpose of the team's work. • Engage employees in productive dialogue. • Ask them what they think. Involve employees in decisions that affect them. • Ask yourself how many of your decisions are *tell, sell, test, consult,* and *join.* How participative is your management style?

Skill:	*Win spiritual commitment.*
Actions:	• Create a sense of connectedness and community. • Demonstrate to employees that you care about their well-being. • Build some social time into the work schedule. • Have some fun together.

Skill:	*Win physical commitment.*
Actions:	• Provide a safe and ergonomically sound work environment. • Promote and support positive health practices. • Make sure that your employees are receiving pay that is comparable to market value and that has internal equity.

Skill:	*Help employees grow.*
Actions:	• Provide ongoing feedback and development tips to team members. • Send your employees to conferences and training seminars. • Support their learning efforts.

Skill:	*Solicit information about how business activities impact people.*
Actions:	• Actively solicit information regarding how business activities and projects are impacting people. • Check in with employees to see how they are doing and how work is affecting their health and their family. • Strive to create reasonable balance between work and life.

Leadership Competency 49:
Building Consensus

Skill: *Create an open and safe environment.*

Actions:
- Use consensus as a process for group decision making when you can honestly support any decision the group makes.
- Respect the thoughts and feelings of others.
- Make sure no one feels threatened.
- Confront behaviors that make others feel uncomfortable.

Skill: *Find common ground.*

Actions:
- Gather and synthesize the input and ideas of all participants.
- Arrive at a decision that is acceptable to all.
- Identify the common values in the group.

Skill: *Think collectively.*

Actions:
- Try not only to achieve better solutions, but also to promote the growth of community and trust.
- Strive to find a solution that everyone thinks is the best solution.

Skill: *Establish egalitarian principles.*

Actions:
- Don't use voting as a way to choose one alternative out of several.
- Use a process to bring many diverse elements together.
- Ask yourself, "Am I taking into account individual feelings and needs?"

Skill: *Create a social order based on honesty and trust.*

Actions:
- Use a qualitative, rather than a quantitative, method of decision making.
- Ask yourself, "Did everyone feel that his or her position was understood and given a proper hearing?"
- Make sure that each person is able to express him- or herself in their own words and of their own will.
- Articulate differences clearly.

Skill: *Stay focused on the vision.*

Actions:
- Define the decisions that need to be made to support the vision.
- Ask yourself, "Is this activity aligned with our future direction?"

Skill: *Resolve conflicts constructively.*

Actions:
- If you are having trouble with a proposal, put forth alternative suggestions.
- Ask yourself, "Am I understanding the other person's point of view?"

Section 3—Building Organizational Capabilities

Leadership Competency 50	Capitalizing on Opportunities
Leadership Competency 51	Networking and Partnering
Leadership Competency 52	Organizational Change
Leadership Competency 53	Organizational Development
Leadership Competency 54	Selecting the Right Talent
Leadership Competency 55	Treating Employees with Dignity and Respect
Leadership Competency 56	Developing Employees
Leadership Competency 57	E-Learning
Leadership Competency 58	Involving Employees
Leadership Competency 59	Empowering Employees
Leadership Competency 60	Recognizing and Rewarding Behaviors and Results
Leadership Competency 61	Retaining Employees
Leadership Competency 62	Succession Planning
Leadership Competency 63	Six Sigma
Leadership Competency 64	Budgeting

Leadership Competency 50: Capitalizing on Opportunities

Skill: *Analyze and prioritize your work responsibilities.*

Actions:
- Analyze your work on a weekly basis and determine your priorities for the upcoming week. Then, for each specific day, plan out the work you want to complete.
- Allow time each day for planning and thinking. Plan tomorrow's activities in detail at the end of each day.

Skill: *Brainstorm how to take advantage of industry trends.*

Actions:
- Develop scenarios for your team or business about what customer and industry conditions you might experience five years from now.
- Brainstorm how your team or business can take advantage of these trends in order to adopt a market leadership role.

Skill: *Brainstorm ways to increase the profitability of your operation.*

Actions:
- Brainstorm ways to increase the profitability of your operation. For brainstorming, use this simple formula: expand, narrow, and choose. First expand options without evaluation. Then narrow choices based on critical criteria. Finally, choose the solution that promises the best payoff.
- After researching the impact of these actions, implement the valuable ideas and track results.

(continued)

Leadership Competency 50:
Capitalizing on Opportunities *(continued)*

Skill: *Clearly communicate project priorities.*

Action: • Make sure to clearly communicate project priorities so that you and your
                 team are always working on the high-impact projects.

Skill: *Conduct a customer survey.*

Actions: • Conduct a customer survey to identify the products/services most needed by
                 your customers.
                 • Ask your customers to give you feedback on the effectiveness, importance,
                 and trends of your services.

Skill: *Demonstrate a "can do" attitude toward meeting challenges.*

Actions: • Always look for possibilities against the backdrop of reality.
                 • It's important to understand the organizational context when presenting
                 solutions.

Skill: *Develop a network of cross-functional contacts for advice.*

Actions: • Develop a network of cross-functional contacts to tap during project
                 execution.
                 • Ask yourself, "What interdependencies are required for successful execution
                 of a given project?"

Skill: *Devote time to planning how to overcome barriers.*

Action: • When faced with internal barriers, set aside time to plan how to overcome
                 these barriers. Internal barriers come in different forms: people, process,
                 product, technology, culture, knowledge, or finance.

Skill: *Identify all possible perspectives and sources of information.*

Action: • When you encounter new or recurring issues or opportunities, determine
                 whether or not you should rely only on the resources and people you are
                 accustomed to using.

Skill: *Make detailed plans so that decisions can be implemented.*

Action: • Practice making detailed plans so that your decisions can be implemented
                 appropriately and with a higher probability of success.

(continued)

Leadership Competency 50:
Capitalizing on Opportunities *(concluded)*

Skill: *Read business publications to keep on top of developments.*

Action: • Read publications such as *Fortune, Business Week,* and *The Wall Street Journal* to keep on top of business developments. Consider the implications of what you are learning for co-workers and customers.

Skill: *Recognize that you will not always have enough information for decision making.*

Actions: • Ask yourself, "Do I have adequate supporting information to make a decision?"
  • Plan what to do if the decision does not generate the results you want.

Skill: *Talk to peers and your management team about their goals and concerns.*

Actions: • Informally talk with your peers and your management team about their goals and concerns.
  • Use this information when you need to link your ideas to their needs.

Skill: *Use an innovative approach to solve a problem in your function.*

Actions: • Choose a problem area in your function that would benefit from an innovative approach.
  • Pull together a team to develop ideas through brainstorming, and decide on a set of plans.
  • Include "breakthrough thinkers" from other groups to add perspective.

Skill: *Work as a consultant on a significant business problem or process.*

Action: • Take on a consultative role in which you must try to solve a significant business problem and/or improve a critical business process by applying problem-solving techniques and using facilitation skills.

Skill: *Work on a project to rebuild a customer relationship.*

Action: • Participate in an effort to address a difficult situation in which the company's reputation is in jeopardy, where you have to help rebuild customer relationships and realign or restructure product or delivery of service.

Skill: *Work on a team to simplify a product or process or improve quality.*

Actions: • Participate on a team that will make a significant contribution toward simplifying the design of a product or a major process; increase the performance or quality of a product or process; or decrease the cost of a product or process.
  • Perform in an assignment that requires you to help analyze and reconfigure an organization's structure, processes, and workforce.

Leadership Competency 51:
Networking and Partnering

Skill: *Develop a systematic approach to networking.*

Action: • Analyze what you need in a network and what you can offer other members.

Skill: *Develop a personal network of contacts to help solve problems.*

Action: • Take personal initiative to develop your own network of contacts with whom you can identify and solve problems and define potential problems, vulnerabilities, and opportunities with product and service offerings.

Skill: *Get involved in supplier relationships in order to improve products or services, cost, or quality.*

Action: • Perform in a role that involves the development of a supplier relationship with another division of the company or outside vendor to improve products, services, cost, or quality.

Skill: *Negotiate an important partnership.*

Action: • Perform in a role that requires you to negotiate important parts of a partnership that will make a significant financial contribution to the overall business (e.g., develop practices or procedures that produce significant improvements in cost, quality, cycle time, or productivity).

Skill: *Serve on cross-functional committees so that you can work with people in other areas.*

Actions: • Identify the groups of people with whom you want to work and develop stronger relationships.
              • Ask yourself what skills you want to develop and who can help you with them.
              • Leverage your experience working in a cross-functional capacity.

Skill: *Keep track of your network.*

Actions: • Create a map of networks, including your "lateral" and "vertical" contacts.
              • List their names, functions, and connections to other important individuals or resources.
              • Update your list and ask yourself what actions you need to take to maintain these relationships.

Skill: *Broaden your scope.*

Actions: • Find ways to strengthen relationships and network outside of your organization.
              • Identify the professional groups, continuing education networks, customer groups, etc., that are important resources or with whom you share interests.
              • Leverage your relationship with these outside sources within your own organization.

Leadership Competency 52: Organizational Change

Skill: *Identify what is going to change.*

Actions:
- Describe to stakeholders the ideal end state and the current state, and explain what people can expect to live through during the change process.
- Clearly state the benefits to the individual and the organization.
- Make it clear what's in it for stakeholders.

Skill: *Identify who is going to be affected.*

Actions:
- Specify the change sponsors, the change agents, and the change targets.
- Clearly define the roles and responsibilities of each constituent.
- Equip the sponsors, change agents, and targets with the tools they need to make the change.

Skill: *Identify how the change will occur.*

Actions:
- Develop the strategies and programs that will get the organization from where it is to where it needs to be.
- Create learning strategies, communication strategies, and reward strategies.

Skill: *Communicate the progress of change in a variety of ways.*

Actions:
- Communicate your vision of the change to others so that they can more easily understand and buy into the change.
- Look for ways to be efficient and capture attention at the same time.
- Plan your communications about change in advance by creating an outline and format. Be sure to ask for feedback.
- Publicize stories of successful change and anecdotal experiences that humanize the process.

Skill: *Create a change-management scorecard.*

Action:
- Create measures of success, and summarize progress against implementation goals, interim results, and other consequences of change.

Skill: *Document any consequences of the change.*

Actions:
- Document any ripple effects or unintended consequences of the change as it is being implemented. The effects or consequences may become as important as the primary change itself.
- Create a formal communication plan to accompany phases and stages of change.

(continued)

Leadership Competency 52:
Organizational Change *(concluded)*

Skill: *During change, communicate much more frequently.*

Actions: • Remember that when it comes to change, it is almost impossible to communicate too much. People hear things at different times, and much of it will be rumor or speculation. Therefore, it is necessary for leaders to communicate the same official message or set of ideas many times and in many different ways so that it is heard and understood.
                • Educate others about change and how people typically react to it.

Skill: *Establish a steering committee for large-scale or long-term change.*

Actions: • Expect resistance to change. Develop strategies to deal with every kind of resistance.
                • Identify the change champions in your organization, and work with them to support and initiate change.
                • Inform customers and suppliers of your significant change initiatives, and ask how this may impact the support they receive from or provide to the organization.

Leadership Competency 53: Organizational Development

Skill: *Improve products and processes.*

Action: • Participate on a team in which you make a significant contribution toward simplifying the design of a product or a major process; increasing the performance or quality of a product or process; or lowering the costs related to a product or process.

Skill: *Contribute to a turnaround.*

Action: • Play a significant role in a situation where the company's reputation is in jeopardy: Perform such activities as assessing a difficult situation and identifying critical issues; raising the level of communication, trust, and teamwork; rebuilding customer relationships; restructuring the team and reconfiguring the product/service delivery approach; taking quick, firm action (including scaling back or "pulling the plug") and making difficult decisions; and rebuilding confidence within the team and with the customer.

Skill: *Develop the workforce.*

Action: • Take the lead in improving the effectiveness of a whole workforce by communicating the critical importance of and leveraging the value of people to the organization; championing the development of a continuous-learning environment; and providing realistic career and professional development alternatives (often in the face of difficult economic and organizational circumstances).

Skill: *Facilitate a strategic planning session.*

Actions: • Work with an executive to conduct an off-site retreat.
                 • Write up the purpose and agenda for the meeting and disseminate it.
                 • Help the team develop or refine its vision, values, mission, goals, and objectives.

Skill: *Conduct a culture audit.*

Actions: • Create a survey instrument by listing the core values and desired norms for the work environment.
                 • Ask for people's perceptions regarding the strength, importance, and direction of the stated norms and values.
                 • Analyze the results and communicate them to the team.

(continued)

Leadership Competency 53:
Organizational Development *(concluded)*

Skill: *Lead a team-building workshop or activity off-site.*

Actions:
- Assess the stage of development, the level of effectiveness, and the degree of virtuality of the team.
- Hold a two-day off-site workshop to clarify direction and to deal with major challenges.
- Facilitate a feedback session in which each member hears about the behaviors that other team members wish he or she would start, stop, or continue.
- Identify communication and decision-making issues, and explore ways to improve.

Skill: *Consult with an executive on a major issue.*

Actions:
- Identify a critical issue a business leader is trying to solve (e.g., how to reduce the time it takes to design and produce new products).
- Work closely with the executive to define the problem, identify the root causes, and generate possible solutions.
- Investigate the strengths and weaknesses in the organization that could impact successful implementation.
- Partner with the executive to ensure that the solution is implemented and that it achieves the desired results.

Skill: *Conduct leadership reviews.*

Actions:
- Identify bench strength for critical jobs in the organization.
- Evaluate each person who is listed in the succession plan on performance, potential, and readiness to move into another job.
- Ask yourself, "Do I have a balanced perspective on strengths and weaknesses, as well as behavior and results?"

Leadership Competency 54:
Selecting the Right Talent

Skill: *Use competency-based hiring and selection tools.*

Action:
- Use appropriate competency-based hiring and selection tools when interviewing candidates in order to improve your overall success rate.

Skill: *Develop a workforce-requirements plan.*

Actions:
- Identify business requirements for the future.
- Determine how those requirements will create new demands for the organization.
- Identify the competencies required to meet those demands.
- Project hiring needs over the next few years.
- Develop a plan to meet those needs.

Skill: *Use multiple sourcing methods.*

Actions:
- Optimize Internet recruiting and broker internal talent.
- Use social networks to do direct recruiting.
- Contact professional associations, universities, and job-placement agencies (particularly if they do minority recruiting).
- Reward employee referrals.

Skill: *Evaluate candidates.*

Actions:
- Use an applicant tracking system for initial assessment.
- Narrow the list of candidates using well-defined predictors of performance excellence.
- Assess functional and technical capabilities, as well as cultural fit, experience, and past performance.
- Use assessment centers to simulate real-life job challenges.

Skill: *Make a compelling offer.*

Actions:
- Address the candidate's key concerns and questions.
- Offer a package that includes compensation, benefits, and career opportunities.
- Match corporate values with the individual's values.
- Explain the economic and social value of accepting the job.
- Articulate the career-value proposition.

Skill: *Engage the new employees quickly and effectively.*

Actions:
- Orient the new colleague to the organizational strategy, structure, and culture.
- Foster a relationship between the new hire and the organization, and facilitate connections with key resources.
- Train the new person in the various technologies required to operate effectively in your work environment.
- Explain career development options to your new colleague.

Leadership Competency 55:
Treating Employees with Dignity and Respect

Skill: *Advocate for diversity.*

Actions:
- Broaden your view of diversity to include significant individual or cultural differences and how they can affect work practices, strategy, and style.
- Challenge assumptions that limit opportunities.
- Challenge organizational policies and practices that might exclude people or groups.
- Develop a network of support for diversity; include colleagues who are interested in working on the positive effects of a more-diverse workforce.
- Explore ideas with each other, and implement them.
- Speak out when it appears that the ideas and contributions of employees who are different from the norm are devalued or ignored.

Skill: *Communicate how behavior affects credibility and effectiveness.*

Action:
- Let people know when their behaviors or values negatively affect their credibility and effectiveness.

Skill: *Conduct a work-environment survey.*

Actions:
- Conduct a work-environment survey, and set up a change team to address the issues.
- Include questions in the survey that relate to employee respect and dignity. For example, ask if employees feel that their opinions count and that they are valued as unique individuals.

Skill: *Do not assume that all people from a particular culture are exactly alike.*

Actions:
- Remember: Individuals see themselves as both part of their culture and different from it.
- Make a point of drawing together diverse groups when discussing issues, solving problems, and developing opportunities.

Skill: *Make sure that the other person knows that you understand their point of view.*

Action:
- When asking someone to explain a point of view different from your own, be sure to say that your intention is to understand that person's viewpoint, not to have him or her justify it.

(continued)

Leadership Competency 55:
Treating Employees with Dignity and Respect *(concluded)*

Skill: *Learn more about other cultures.*

Actions:
- Learn more about other cultures and their belief systems through travel, books, films, and conversations and by attending local cultural events and celebrations.
- Monitor yourself to detect any incorrect or inappropriate assumptions you subconsciously make or stereotypical ways you respond to other people.

Skill: *Partner with an individual whose experiences are different from your own.*

Action:
- Partner with an individual whose background and experiences are different from your own, and agree to learn and then teach each other one or two skills that will improve performance in some way.

Skill: *Give feedback that is specific and behavioral.*

Actions:
- Practice giving feedback that is specific and behavioral.
- When your partner achieves a goal or completes work, make sure to give positive feedback to reinforce the behavior. (Avoid feedback that is judgmental.)

Skill: *Seek to understand diversity from a global perspective.*

Actions:
- Seek to understand diversity from a global, as well as a national perspective, if appropriate to your business and location.
- Question your own cultural values and background and learn more about it to gain a better appreciation for how these things influence your decision-making style, values, and reactions to different views.
- Speak slowly and use easier vocabulary when communicating with people for whom English is only a second language so that they can more easily understand and offer their own thoughts.
- Take a course in cross-cultural studies to understand culture and its impact on people.

Skill: *Use personality tools such as the Myers-Briggs Type Indicator to better understand differences among people.*

Action:
- Use personality tools such as the Myers-Briggs Type Indicator (MBTI) to learn ways of understanding individual differences.

Leadership Competency 56:
Developing Employees

Skill: *Gauge readiness.*

Action: • Assess whether or not the individual is ready for training. If the person is not ready because of insufficient motivation or urgency, make readiness the focus of intervention efforts.

Skill: *Identify competencies required for success.*

Actions: • Analyze the business requirements for the future.
              • Ask yourself, "What demands will these requirements place on the organization?"
              • Identify which competencies will be required to meet those demands in the areas of leadership, marketing, sales, human resources, information resources, law, investor relations, development, and operations at all levels of the organization.

Skill: *Provide feedback on competencies.*

Actions: • Identify the competencies required for success in each job.
              • Provide a 360° feedback mechanism for employees so that they can obtain confidential, multi-source feedback on the competencies required in their current job and the job to which they aspire.
              • Provide confidential reports to employees that indicate the gap between current proficiency, required proficiency, as well as information on strengths and developmental opportunities.

Skill: *Encourage employees to create individual development plans.*

Actions: • Make employee development an essential part of the performance management system.
              • Provide a balanced scorecard for employees that gives them feedback on how they contribute to financial viability, customer service, business process improvement, and self-development.
              • Support the implementation of individual development plans.

Skill: *Support learning efforts.*

Actions: • Encourage employees to attend courses, take advantage of e-learning programs, and read professional books and journals.
              • Hold lunch-and-learn sessions.
              • Ask yourself, "Which projects could we conduct a postmortem or review session that would yield a rich source of learning?"
              • Encourage knowledge-sharing by creating an expert resource network.
              • Participate in seminars and Webinars.
              • Demonstrate your own commitment to learning.

(continued)

Leadership Competency 56:
Developing Employees *(concluded)*

Skill: *Develop an employment-focused Web site to broadcast openings.*

Actions:
- Develop an employment-focused Web site to broadcast openings to a wider number and different set of potential employees.
- Include candidate profiling as part of the site to help you sift through the large numbers of candidates.

Skill: *Develop performance management systems that support business strategies.*

Actions:
- Use a balanced scorecard approach in which the employee sets goals and gets feedback on financial metrics, customer relationships, process improvement, and learning and development.
- Make sure that employees are rewarded for implementing their individual development plan.

Skill: *Monitor employee trends in your industry.*

Actions:
- Monitor trends in your industry to determine which competencies and knowledge will become increasingly important.
- Make sure your organization has employees with these competencies: Hire them externally or train your current employees.

Leadership Competency 57:
E-Learning

Skill: *Take an online learning course.*

Actions:
- Inquire about the different online courses available to you.
- Pick a competency that you need to improve.
- Select an online course that will help you improve that competency.
- Upon completion, ask yourself, "What were the advantages and disadvantages of this online class, compared to classroom training?"

Skill: *Participate in a cyberspace classroom.*

Actions:
- Sign up for a class that is being taught on the Web.
- Learn the different ways you can ask and respond to questions in cyberspace.

Skill: *Become a virtual student.*

Actions:
- Use the Internet as a source of information for questions that arise.
- Inquire about distance learning opportunities offered by universities.
- For any source of information on the Internet, ask yourself, "How reliable is this information? Can I find corroborating validation?"

Skill: *Build a "virtual learning" community.*

Actions:
- Investigate different electronic team rooms and learning-management systems.
- Create an electronic workspace, and ask colleagues to join.
- Define the purpose of the space, the participants, and the categories of work you want to address in the workspace.

Skill: *Design a Web-based training program.*

Actions:
- Work with an instructional designer to build a Web-based training program.
- Learn how to use Web-X or Placeware.
- Use the technology to deliver a training program to your colleagues who work in different locations and time zones.

Skill: *Evaluate the cost-effectiveness of different learning strategies.*

Actions:
- Do an analysis of how much you are spending on all of your learning and training programs.
- Categorize the programs into *e-learning, classroom, self-paced,* etc.
- Evaluate the results of those programs.
- Determine the most cost-effective way to deliver each training program.

Skill: *Create a blended learning solution.*

Actions:
- Incorporate e-learning into traditional classroom training.
- Ask yourself, "What content can I deliver in an e-learning format before and after the classroom training to improve the effectiveness and reduce costs?"

Leadership Competency 58: Involving Employees

Skill: *Establish meeting policies that "pull" for participation.*

Action:
- Establish meeting policies and practices that mandate collaboration and include the full participation of everyone.

Skill: *Create a suggestion program.*

Actions:
- Explore new software programs that help to stimulate and organize employee suggestions.
- Send out the message that you welcome suggestions and want to hear ideas for improvement.
- Ask yourself, "How often do I act on ideas suggested by others? What kind of feedback do I give to people who suggest solutions?"

Skill: *Encourage idea generation.*

Actions:
- Ask people to contribute their ideas concerning problems the company is facing.
- Hold brainstorming sessions.
- Ask for input during meetings.
- Ask yourself, "How much meeting time do I devote to gathering information from others and collaborative problem solving?"

Skill: *Create a safe, supportive environment.*

Actions:
- Ask yourself, "How safe do people feel to speak up in my organization?"
- Conduct a culture audit that asks how well the organization supports respect and inclusiveness.

Skill: *Free initiative and creativity.*

Actions:
- Encourage employees to take the initiative.
- Identify your exemplars and give them more freedom.
- Ask yourself, "How much do I try to control behavior vs. leave people alone?"

Skill: *See employees as reservoirs of knowledge and wisdom.*

Actions:
- Challenge your assumptions and beliefs about people. Do you see them as problems to be managed or potential to be tapped?
- Ask yourself, "How are my beliefs and assumptions influencing the conclusions I am making about my colleagues?"

(continued)

Leadership Competency 58:
Involving Employees (concluded)

Skill: *Invite employees to talk with you.*

Actions: • Walk the halls.
               • Ask people what they are working on.
               • Hold breakfast meetings with random groups of employees to listen to their concerns and ideas.

Skill: *Ask people what they think.*

Actions: • Give people a chance to tell you what they think.
               • When an issue arises, ask for input and suggestions.
               • Ask yourself, "How often do I ask others for solutions and ideas?"

Skill: *Think interdependently.*

Actions: • Actively seek ways to help your colleagues succeed.
               • Ask yourself, "Am I an independent thinker, or an *inter*dependent thinker?"
               • Strive to improve collaboration in the team by working with others.
               • Try to avoid making unilateral decisions.

Skill: *Identify your own leadership style.*

Actions: • Analyze your decisions on the following scale: *tell, sell, test, consult,* and *join.* How many of your decisions are imposed without input (tell)? How many decisions are made collaboratively, with equal weight for all (consult)?
               • Ask yourself, "Is there a reasonable balance of decisions along the scale?"

Skill: *Support community involvement.*

Actions: • Develop cross-functional employee involvement initiatives that directly support business goals and community needs.
               • Assess employee interests, company needs, and community needs.
               • Provide incentives for employees to participate.
               • Create two-way communication concerning employee involvement in the community.

Leadership Competency 59: Empowering Employees

Skill: *Provide direction.*

Actions:
- Communicate the mission, goals, objectives, and strategic direction of the organization.
- Clarify expectations for results and behaviors.
- Establish clear boundaries and parameters for decision making.

Skill: *Provide autonomy.*

Actions:
- Free exemplars to initiate in ways that are consistent with the strategic direction and within established boundaries and parameters.
- Encourage risk taking and initiative. Give people room to be creative.

Skill: *Provide support.*

Actions:
- Make discriminations about how much support each employee will need for success. Some employees may need more coaching and direction than others.
- Assess what kind of resources will be required for the employee or team to be successful.
- Engage employees in productive dialogue about the time, money, tools, and technology that will be required to implement their ideas.

Skill: *Emphasize professional development.*

Actions:
- Encourage employees to develop themselves by providing training and learning opportunities.
- Become a role model for professional development by openly learning and pursuing new skills yourself.
- Find ways to connect employees with important learning opportunities, and follow up with them.
- Look for ways to acknowledge and credit people for improving themselves and making valuable contributions.

Leadership Competency 60:
Recognizing and Rewarding Behaviors and Results

Skill: *Lead a team in the development of a reward-and-recognition system.*

Actions:
- Head up a team charged with developing a reward-and-recognition system, career development methods and structures, or similar effort.
- Find out what kinds of rewards your employees value that you might provide.

Skill: *Show that you have a positive attitude.*

Actions:
- Demonstrate a "can-do" attitude related to problem solving and meeting challenges.
- When faced with challenges, always look for possibilities against the backdrop of reality.
- Consider the organizational context when presenting solutions.
- Remember: A positive attitude is a reward in itself.

Skill: *Develop a team-feedback approach.*

Actions:
- Create a system for providing constructive feedback to one another.
- Ask each person to critique themselves, then their team members, and finally you.
- Be aware of how well each person is able to recognize excellent performance when they see it and how interpersonally skilled each is at giving feedback.
- Keep the conversation behavioral and non-judgmental.
- Work with the team so that you can all recognize excellent performance.

Skill: *Prioritize what is important.*

Actions:
- Spend time prioritizing what is important and what results you would like to achieve.
- Apply the prioritization process: List the organization's objectives, and then list what you want to achieve in that context.
- Recognize and reward progress toward those objectives.

Skill: *Help your team members meet their objectives.*

Action:
- Learn the difference between participating (doing what's asked), contributing (adding value to the task), and leadership (adding value to others in order to achieve success).

Skill: *Match rewards and recognition to level of functioning.*

Action:
- Assess your employees on the following scale: 1 = *detractor;* 2 = *observer;* 3 = *participant;* 4 = *contributor;* 5 = *leader.* When recognizing and rewarding performance, remember that people at different levels of functioning need different types of rewards and recognition. A leader wants more challenging work and freedom to initiate. A detractor needs a "full hearing" from you to understand the source of their negativity and be able to look for resolution.

Leadership Competency 61: Retaining Employees

Skill: *Foster a positive relationship with the employee.*

Actions:
- Inquire about the employee's interests and values.
- Ask questions about their personal life and career aspirations.
- Ask yourself, "How much do I know about my colleagues?"
- Show that you care about the employee's well-being by being flexible with work schedules and encouraging participation in wellness activities.

Skill: *Support opportunities for learning and development.*

Actions:
- Provide budget support for external courses, and allow time to participate in internal courses.
- Encourage interactions with customers and cross-functional teams.
- Create an expert resource network and other databases that enable knowledge sharing.
- Model learning and development by implementing your own personal development plan.
- Encourage participation in seminars and Webinars.

Skill: *Support work-life balance.*

Actions:
- Have conversations with your employees about personal interests and issues.
- Listen to concerns about child care or elder care issues. If possible, allow flexible work arrangements so that employees can attend to personal as well as work issues in the most effective and humane ways.

Skill: *Provide meaningful work.*

Actions:
- Ask employees about their personal values and career objectives.
- Look for opportunities for employees to engage in work that satisfies their values and moves them toward their career objectives.
- Encourage employees to get involved in community projects or groups who are making important contributions.

Skill: *Involve employees in decision making.*

Actions:
- List the decisions you make in a given day.
- Ask yourself, "Did I ignore people in making this decision? Or did I simply inform them of the decision after the fact?"
- Look for opportunities to involve colleagues in a meaningful way in decisions that affect them.
- Explore ways to incorporate their thinking and behavior into your plans.
- Think about what it would take to inspire employees to perform at their highest levels.

(continued)

Leadership Competency 61:
Retaining Employees *(concluded)*

Skill: *Link employee values to the company vision and values.*

Actions:
- Articulate and communicate the company vision, mission, and core values.
- Ask employees which of these values are most important to them.
- Ask yourself how inspirational and aspirational the vision and values are to you and your colleagues.
- Listen to your employees to understand what is important to them. Then provide opportunities for employees to connect their individual values with the organization's values.

Skill: *Provide adequate rewards and recognition.*

Actions:
- Assess the level of functioning of each person on your team on the following scale: *detractor, observer, participant, contributor,* or *leader.*
- Ask yourself, "What rewards and recognition strategies work for people at each level of functioning?"
- Expand the options you have for rewarding and recognizing people.
- Read a book on the subject to get ideas.
- Personalize your rewards and recognition strategies by linking them to what is motivating or important to individual colleagues.

Leadership Competency 62:
Succession Planning

Skill: *Assess bench strength for key jobs.*

Actions:
- Review all managers on performance, potential, and readiness.
- Rate performance based on contribution and leadership.
- Ask yourself, "Has this person exceeded expectations on the current job? And has she or he promoted self-development and core values?"
- Rate individual potential on capability and commitment.
- Ask yourself, "Does this person have the knowledge, skills, and experience to do more? And is this person committed to the company?"
- Decide if the person is ready to assume a bigger role now or within the next year.

Skill: *Identify and use the talent pool for all key job openings.*

Actions:
- Whenever a key position opens up, go first to the talent pool.
- Review the list of high-potential, high-performing people who are ready to move now.
- Consider those candidates first for significant job opportunities.

Skill: *Encourage all people in the talent pool to create development plans.*

Actions:
- Invite all high-potential, high-performing people to apply for developmental opportunities.
- Develop a set of criteria and a process for awarding these opportunities.
- Decide on a number of educational opportunities to be granted each year (e.g., a six-month Harvard Executive Education Program).
- Encourage all people in the talent pool to create development plans.

Skill: *Conduct annual reviews of performance and succession possibilities.*

Actions:
- Meet with your team to review the criteria and the process.
- Rate each manager on performance, potential, and readiness.
- Review the list of key positions, and search the talent pool for people who might be ready to move into a high-impact job.

Leadership Competency 63:
Six Sigma

Skill: *Define Six Sigma elements.*

Actions: • Communicate the definition of quality: Meeting commitments in accordance with requirements.
• Discuss the subject of adult learning principles with the team.
• Clarify roles and responsibilities, introduce basic statistics, and provide an overview of change leadership.

Skill: *Measure results achieved.*

Actions: • Conduct project reviews to make sure that adequate progress is being made.
• Create process maps to clearly articulate how work gets done.
• Provide cause-and-effect tools. Conduct project planning and capability analysis.

Skill: *Analyze data.*

Actions: • Learn how to do graphical data analysis.
• Take an online course in statistics to learn how to determine sample sizes and conduct regression and analysis of variance.

Skill: *Continuously improve.*

Actions: • Conduct regular project reviews to determine what is working and what is not working. Invite suggestions for improvement.
• Reward ideas that produce significant results.
• Look for ways to improve transactions as well as operating procedures.

Skill: *Control for variance.*

Actions: • Learn statistical process control.
• Explore ways to eliminate any variance in project deliverables.

Skill: *Manage team dynamics.*

Actions: • Pay attention to how the team is interacting.
• Identify interdependencies both within the team and between organizations.
• Bring the team together to improve ways of working together to achieve common goals.

Skill: *Identify variables.*

Actions: • Identify the variables that could impact success.
• Look for input variables, processing variables, output variables, and feedback variables.
• Bring the team together to improve input, process, output, and feedback.

(continued)

Leadership Competency 63:
Six Sigma *(concluded)*

Skill: *Present results.*

Actions:
- Summarize the results of the Six Sigma effort.
- Put together a presentation that highlights achievements.
- Involve the team in the presentation. Prepare and present the results to upper management.

Leadership Competency 64:
Budgeting

Skill: *Identify sources of income.*

Actions: • Identify sources of income by category: sales, allocations, charge backs, etc.
               • Ask yourself, "How sure am I that this income will occur?"
               • Assign a probability.

Skill: *Identify expense categories.*

Actions: • Create categories for all expenses: wages, travel, utilities, rent, supplies, education, etc.
               • Review previous budgets to make sure you have thought of all possible expenses.

Skill: *Estimate revenues.*

Action: • Forecast your revenues for the year. These revenues could include your allocation for the year, as well as charge backs, sales, interest, and dividends.

Skill: *Estimate expenses.*

Actions: • Anticipate all expenses that you might have over the year.
               • Try to be as accurate as possible.
               • Be careful to think of all possible expenses in advance.

Skill: *Set targets and goals.*

Actions: • After you have forecasted income and anticipated expenses, set targets for each month of the year.
               • Ask yourself, "Do I have an income-and-expense goal for each month?"

Skill: *Track revenues and expenses.*

Actions: • Monitor revenues and expenses monthly.
               • Make sure you get accurate reports that allow you to see how you are doing.
               • Prepare a report that shows budget-to-actual each month for every line item.

Skill: *Analyze the budget.*

Actions: • Study revenues and expense variances.
               • Identify gaps and probe for root causes.
               • Inform everyone who is involved in your budget how they are doing in relation to the budget.
               • Let people know that you expect everyone to help you manage the budget.

(continued)

Leadership Competency 64:
Budgeting *(concluded)*

Skill: *Brainstorm ways to improve.*

Actions:
- Bring together your team to explore ways to increase revenue and to reduce costs.
- Look for new ways to beat the budget.

Skill: *Make modifications.*

Actions:
- Consider the budget as a dynamic document.
- Make changes during the year in response to changing conditions. If you change any line item of the budget, make sure you communicate the changes to everyone in your department.
- Develop a thoughtful budget planning process so that there is ample time for input and analysis.

Section 4—Building Customer Relationships and Capabilities:

Leadership Competency 65	Customer Service
Leadership Competency 66	Customer Focus
Leadership Competency 67	Efficiency Orientation
Leadership Competency 68	Building Partnerships

Leadership Competency 65: Customer Service

Skill: *Serve as a role model for customer service.*

Action:
- Fully explain and communicate to your employees your commitment to high standards of customer service. Then, be a good customer-service role model.

Skill: *Create a monthly newsletter for internal communication.*

Action:
- Create a monthly internal newsletter that includes the following: tips on how to deal with customer requests and complaints, customer-focused policies and procedures, summaries of new books and articles on customer service, and names of individuals who are providing excellent customer service.

Skill: *Develop standards for products/services that meet customer requirements.*

Actions:
- Develop standards for customer service that exceed customer expectations.
- Identify and challenge critical factors that hinder even greater performance, quality, or customer service.

Skill: *Seek feedback from your customers.*

Actions:
- Remember that all customers want to be heard.
- Design feedback systems tailored to each customer segment, and ask the right questions to get the information you need.
- Welcome critical comments: Customers who take time to give you feedback are sending the message that they want the relationship to work.
- Check back regularly to see how things are going after you have responded to a customer's comment.
- Treat customers' perceptions as reality; they are, in fact, reality for your customer.

(continued)

Leadership Competency 65:
Customer Service *(continued)*

Skill:	*Deliver on your customer commitments.*

Actions:
- Know your customer's requirements.
- Be sure you understand the commitments you have made by knowing when, what, how, where, how many, to whom, etc.
- Communicate the commitments to your team and the context for those who may not deal directly with the customer: Why does the customer need it this way? And what are the consequences for them if we fail to deliver?

Skill:	*Train for customer focus.*

Actions:
- Hire the best people for customer service. While training them, treat employees the way you expect them to treat customers.
- Provide an orientation to each part of your business so that employees understand what it takes to meet customer requirements at every step of the process.
- Involve customer service "stars" in the training; have them talk about and demonstrate the best possible practices.

Skill:	*Set high standards for customer service.*

Actions:
- Create a statement that encompasses your service commitment and defines it in terms of both employee and customer expectations.
- Make sure it is concise and compelling.
- Demonstrate customer focus throughout the organization, and use cross-functional teams to improve work processes to more clearly meet customer requirements.
- Conduct a benchmarking visit with organizations that are known for their superior customer service.

Skill:	*Work together to serve the customer.*

Actions:
- Remember that everyone in the organization can provide important feedback on how to meet customer needs and create more loyal customer relationships.
- Use e-mail or groupware to gather information from employees about what customers are saying or feeling about service.
- Conduct periodic integration meetings with people who work with a specific customer, and brainstorm ways to integrate their work/services. Give your customers the impression that different teams in the organization work together seamlessly.

(continued)

Leadership Competency 65:
Customer Service *(concluded)*

Skill: *Recover from mistakes.*

Actions:
- Don't wait for the customer to come to you with a problem.
- If you are aware of a problem, be the first to contact your customer—emphasizing a "no-surprises" motto.
- Take full responsibility, and don't blame another for the mistake or problem; your customer only cares about how the problem will be resolved—not who caused it. Remember: Sometimes a good recovery can make your relationship with the customer even stronger.

Leadership Competency 66:
Customer Focus

Skill: *Collaborate with a team of representative customers to develop business strategies that meet mutual needs.*

Actions: • Help customers understand the company's products.
                • Map key processes with a customer team.
                • Participate in customer problem-solving meetings. Spend time working in your customer's area.

Skill: *Develop profiles of key accounts.*

Action: • Develop profiles of all key accounts: key contacts, office hours, potential staff contacts, etc. (Consider use of a Web-based tracking system to profile accounts—such as Salesforce.com.)

Skill: *Stay laser-focused on the customer.*

Actions: • Perform a customer needs analysis.
                • Formulate customer-specific pre- and post-call plans into daily plans.
                • Use specific targeted selling messages in sales calls.

Leadership Competency 67:
Efficiency Orientation

Skill: *Develop measurements for the implementation of new products/services.*

Action: • Develop measurements for the implementation of new products/services.

Skill: *Create an on-demand workplace.*

Actions:
• Bring together all the strands of information that run through the workplace.
• Simplify and integrate core processes.
• Standardize as many processes as you can.

Skill: *Manage interruptions.*

Actions:
• Schedule time in your day for meetings and phone calls.
• Let people know when you are available for meetings and when you are not.
• Ask yourself, "How often do I get distracted by an unplanned event and waste a lot of time?"

Skill: *Prioritize and stick to goals.*

Actions:
• Write down your most important priorities each day.
• Put your priorities in order of importance and urgency.
• Check each one off as you complete it.
• Stay focused on your priorities until you finish your list for the day.

Skill: *Organize electronic documents.*

Actions:
• Create folders on your computer that help you organize your work.
• Place all documents related to your projects in the respective folders.
• Ask yourself, "How easily can I find electronic documents that I have filed?"
• Take time to think about the best way to organize your electronic documents.

Leadership Competency 68:
Building Partnerships

Skill: *Create a partnership agreement.*

Actions: • Define the level of relationship you want to form: vendor relationship, preferred provider, or trusted advisor.
                • Be clear about what you want from the partnership, and how you will measure its success.

Skill: *Choose a business structure.*

Actions: • After agreeing on a shared vision, decide what kind of structure is required: a corporation, limited liability, or a contractual agreement.
                • Define terms and conditions in advance.

Skill: *Name the purpose of the partnership.*

Actions: • Ask yourself, "Why are we forming this partnership?"
                • Define levels of authority and responsibility.
                • Write a statement of purpose.

Skill: *Define respective contributions and expectations.*

Actions: • Develop a contract with your partner.
                • Define roles and responsibilities.
                • Ask yourself, "Am I clear about the expectations of all parties involved?"

Skill: *Get the partnership started.*

Actions: • Identify key process interfaces, and develop them.
                • Set up bookkeeping and accounting procedures.
                • Develop a budget, and communicate it.
                • Negotiate unsettled terms and conditions.

Chapter 3: Driving
The Third Meta-Competency

Introduction

Unfortunately, it is not enough to identify strategic opportunities and develop the capabilities to capitalize on them. Leaders must drive for results. The capability to perform all three meta-competencies at high levels is what distinguishes great leadership from mediocre leadership. **Driving for results means that the leader is able to align people, processes, technology, rewards, metrics, and culture with the strategy.**

This chapter is divided into three sections:

Section 1 Applying Skills
Section 2 Managing for Results
Section 3 Achieving Profitability

Applying skills means that all leadership competencies are used appropriately in a variety of situations. Great leaders make fine discriminations as to what skills to use and when to use them. Getting outstanding results requires unrelenting attention to customer needs, as well as the ability to build partnerships, make timely and accurate decisions, solve problems, delegate work, oversee marketing campaigns, and mediate conflicts.

Managing for results means doing whatever it takes to achieve performance goals and objectives. Whatever it takes means actively managing: people and their careers, meetings, projects, quality, teams, conflicts, crises, diversity, knowledge, and business operations. Results don't happen by wishing them to happen. Getting great results requires tremendous discipline regarding the best management practices and continuous rigor regarding the methodologies required for high performance.

Achieving profitability means staying vigilant on revenues and expenses and making sure everyone is meeting their goals and managing their budgets. It means holding people accountable for their commitments, aligning the culture with the strategic direction, re-engineering processes based on new information and conditions in the marketplace, selling effectively, and competing well. Great leaders achieve profitability by having high expectations, demanding excellence, and driving for results. All of this needs to be accomplished without jeopardizing human and organizational capital.

And that's the differentiating characteristic of great leaders: They are able to build financial capital as a result of their ability to focus on all forms of capital development simultaneously: information capital, human capital, organizational capital, customer capital, and community capital.

Section 1—Applying Skills

Leadership Competency 69	Decision Making
Leadership Competency 70	Problem Solving
Leadership Competency 71	Marketing
Leadership Competency 72	Delegating
Leadership Competency 73	Communicating Across Cultures
Leadership Competency 74	Servicing Internal Customers
Leadership Competency 75	Mediating

Leadership Competency 69: Decision Making

Skill: *Generate a range of what-if scenarios when addressing problems.*

Actions:
- Develop what-if scenarios for various decision paths.
- Discuss the tradeoffs for different decisions with a trusted peer.

Skill: *Determine criteria.*

Actions:
- Expand the values and/or objectives that the decision in question will address.
- Write definitions for each of the criteria.

Skill: *Weight criteria.*

Action:
- Weight the values and objectives, and use them as criteria for the effectiveness of the decision *(How well will this decision satisfy these criteria?).*

Skill: *Expand alternatives.*

Actions:
- Brainstorm all the decision alternatives that could be made. Don't restrict yourself at this point to decisions you think will "work."
- Think speculatively.

Skill: *Seek out all information that relates to the issue.*

Actions:
- Use the grid you have created (alternatives by criteria) as a guide to gather the input and information you will need in order to make a decision.
- Ask yourself, "Have I explored multiple sources of information?"
- Be as open and rigorous as you believe the decision requires.

(continued)

Leadership Competency 69:
Decision Making *(concluded)*

Skill:	*Compare alternatives.*
Actions:	• Using the decision information you generated, compare each alternative by assessing how well it satisfies your criteria.
	• For each cell, ask whether the decision would be a plus, a minus, or a neutral for that criteria.

Skill:	*Select the best alternative.*
Action:	• After completing your grid (alternatives by criteria), add up the columns to see which alternative best satisfies your criteria. You may need to use your weights to differentiate one alternative from another. Remember: Using a scoring system will help you make an informed decision; it does not imply that you should accept or reject any particular alternative.

Skill:	*Explore ways to improve the alternative.*
Actions:	• After you have made your decision, review your grid of alternatives and criteria to see if one or more alternatives satisfies particular criteria better than the one you selected.
	• Ask yourself, "Is there a way I can use aspects of other alternatives to satisfy my criteria more fully?"

Skill:	*Communicate your decision.*
Actions:	• After you have reached what you believe to be the best decision, make sure you communicate it clearly and consistently to all people who are affected by it.
	• Ask yourself, "Who needs to know about this decision? And what is the best way to communicate it?" Just as you were thorough in thinking through the decision, it is equally important to be thorough in thinking through how it gets communicated (e.g., e-mail, meeting, face-to-face, etc.).

Leadership Competency 70: Problem Solving

Skill: *Review failed problem-solving interventions.*

Action:
- Review problem-solving interventions that failed in order to develop improved strategies.

Skill: *Define the problem.*

Actions:
- Solicit input about causes and solutions from a wide range of contacts (e.g., customers, peers, mentors).
- List all the ways the problem manifests itself.
- Create a concise problem definition that is stated, if possible, in mathematical terms (i.e., our current capabilities < required capabilities).

Skill: *Identify the root causes.*

Actions:
- List all the possible causes of the problem.
- Use fishbone analysis to categorize possible problems as people, process, technology, culture, knowledge, or strategy.
- Conduct Pareto analysis to determine which of the possible causes account for 80 percent of the variance.

Skill: *Expand possible solutions.*

Actions:
- Brainstorm all possible ways to solve this problem.
- Make sure that the solutions address the root causes of the problem.
- Encourage non-conventional, non-routine thinking to solve the problem.

Skill: *Apply decision-making skills to determine the best solution.*

Action:
- Define the criteria for selecting the best option. Then weight the criteria in terms of importance, compare each alternative against the criteria, and choose the best solution.

Skill: *Test your concerns, ideas, and solutions with team members.*

Actions:
- List all the positive and negative implications of the solution.
- Identify ways to overcome the negative implications.
- Involve others in developing the plan and implementing the solution.

Leadership Competency 71:
Marketing

Skill: *Begin with client problems and needs.*

Actions: • Ask your customers what their primary concerns are. What are the business
                  problems they are trying to solve?
                • Ask yourself, "What needs do my solutions meet? What would be the result of
                  my product, service, or solution?"

Skill: *Create a value proposition.*

Actions: • Identify the benefits of your products, services, or solutions to the customer.
                • Let them sample the product.
                • Ask your customer, "What is the fundamental need or objective that drives
                  the decision to use your products, services, or solution?"

Skill: *Develop and maintain your network of relationships.*

Actions: • Develop a relationship with every customer as their trusted advisor.
                • Use a database to organize client information and track customer contact.
                • Ask, "What can I do to build new relationships?"

Skill: *Create an integrated marketing solution.*

Actions: • Make every aspect of your business about marketing.
                • Make everyone responsible for marketing your products, services, and
                  solutions.
                • Create a master plan that integrates all of your marketing programs.
                • Ask yourself, "How clear am I about my marketing responsibilities?"

Skill: *Generate demand and opportunities.*

Actions: • Make it an ongoing effort to identify and test new market opportunities that
                  could create continued business growth.
                • Create a strategy for a new product, service, solution, or marketing idea.
                  Cross-market your products, services, and solutions to your customers.
                • Ask yourself, "Which idea offers the most market potential?"

Skill: *Set goals.*

Actions: • Define specific goals for your marketing efforts.
                • Ask yourself, "How much time do I allocate for marketing, versus the other
                  functions of my business?"
                • Pick one urgent objective that can be accomplished within the next month,
                  and use existing resources to achieve it.
                • Decide who will do what by when.

(continued)

Leadership Competency 71:
Marketing *(concluded)*

Skill: *Test and assess your results.*

Actions:
- Determine the results of your marketing efforts, and compare them to other alternatives.
- Ask yourself, "How effective is our current marketing strategy?"
- Try new ideas and variables to increase effectiveness.

Leadership Competency 72:
Delegating

Skill:	*Define the task.*
Actions:	• Define and clarify the task you are planning to delegate, and assess the degree of difficulty and importance of the task. • Review your list of goals, objectives, and tasks. Identify those tasks that you can't do, those you don't want to do, and those that seem inappropriate for you to do given your level and experience. • Ask yourself, "Which of these tasks are necessary or desirable for someone else to do and that present a developmental opportunity for them?" Remember, some tasks may need to be delegated, even if they are not developmental.

Skill:	*Assess commitment and capability.*
Actions:	• For each task that you want to delegate, list the people you are considering for the task. Assess each person's commitment and capability for doing the task. • Ask yourself, "Will this person be motivated to do this task? Does this person have the knowledge, skills, and experience to perform the task successfully?"

Skill:	*Assess the need for coaching, direction, and support.*
Action:	• Given the importance and urgency of the task and the commitment and capability of the person to whom you are delegating the task, assess how much coaching, direction, and support you will need to provide in order to meet an acceptable standard of performance.

Skill:	*Select the best person for the task.*
Actions:	• Based on your assessment of the individuals and the task, decide to whom you will delegate the task. Meet with this person to discuss the task. • Get their commitment, provide direction, and ask how they would like to be supported. • Clarify how available you will be to help, and how much authority the person has to act.

Skill:	*Ask for progress reports.*
Actions:	• Meet with the individual as often as necessary to ensure successful completion of the task. • Ask yourself, "Have I provided sufficient direction, autonomy, and support?" • Depending on the importance and urgency of the task, ask for regular progress reports to ensure that milestones are being met according to an agreed upon timeline.

(continued)

Leadership Competency 72:
Delegating *(concluded)*

Skill: *Reward achievement.*

Actions:
- Upon successful completion of the task, think about the most appropriate reward or recognition.
- Ask yourself, "What would this person most value?" Depending on the answer to that question, decide which reward would be most appropriate (e.g., a simple thank-you, more work, a gift certificate, or some monetary compensation).

Leadership Competency 73:
Communicating Across Cultures

Skill: *See all cultures as compartmentalized societies.*

Action:
- Recognize that people within a nation can be more different from one another than people across national cultures.

Skill: *Establish criteria to determine which abilities or skills a person needs in order to acquire "intercultural competence."*

Actions:
- Take into account personality, skills, and knowledge.
- Ask yourself, "Is this person open-minded, persistent, adaptive, resilient, creative, and patient?"
- Assess the individual's ability to relate cross-culturally, think systematically, and plan globally.
- Consider what knowledge the person lacks in history, social psychology, and anthropology that is relevant to your company's needs.

Skill: *Identify the barriers that cultural differences can construct.*

Actions:
- List the opportunities and challenges related to participation, problem solving, rewards, learning styles, communication, and trust.
- Develop strategies for dealing with all of those potential barriers. Remember that different cultures have different expectations or ideas about commitment, contribution, confrontation, confidentiality, and competitiveness.

Skill: *Identify cultural self-perceptions.*

Actions:
- Identify the ways in which you identify with your cultural community.
- Describe your own cultural community, and assess the strength of your identification.

Skill: *Identify cultural presuppositions.*

Actions:
- Increase your awareness of how people outside your own social community are characterized negatively on the basis of someone else's values.
- Ask yourself how often you characterize another culture as "inadequate" and your own culture as "ideal."

Skill: *Respect differences in experience.*

Actions:
- Increase your understanding of how the same message can be interpreted several different ways, depending on life experiences, position, etc.
- Recognize that social positions are created in social structures.

Leadership Competency 74:
Servicing Internal Customers

Skill: *Understand your customer's needs.*

Actions:
- Listen to the customer, and establish yourself as a trusted advisor.
- Demonstrate your credibility by doing what you say you will do.

Skill: *Demonstrate commitment to your customer.*

Actions:
- Be accessible and available. Respond quickly to requests.
- Demonstrate knowledge of the customer's concerns.
- Resolve issues quickly and fairly.
- Ask your customer, "How am I doing?"
- Deliver what you promise.

Skill: *Earn credibility and trust from your customer.*

Actions:
- Communicate genuinely with the customer.
- Demonstrate your capabilities by showing how you can help your customers achieve their goals.

Skill: *Counsel your customer.*

Actions:
- Do not engage in dominant or deceitful behaviors.
- Engage in productive dialogue with your customer by getting their perspective, giving your perspective, merging images, and then elevating the discussion.
- Ask questions that lead to discovery and reflection.
- Ask yourself, "Do I help my customer generate options?"

Skill: *Add value to the customer.*

Actions:
- Provide a vital service to the customer.
- Help the customer become an expert in a given area.
- Identify thought leaders who can expand your customer's thinking.

Skill: *Develop a partnership with your customer.*

Actions:
- Read a book on how to become a trusted advisor.
- Define the level at which your customer would rate your partnership.
- Define where you want to be on the scale.
- Identify two things that you can do within the next two weeks to "scale up" your customer's perception.
- Develop your skills of positioning, contracting, and engaging in productive dialogue.

Leadership Competency 75:
Mediating

Skill: *Identify the dispute.*

Actions: • Clarify the conflict situation and the dispute.
                • Ask yourself if you understand the root causes of the dispute from each person's perspective.

Skill: *Prepare for the meeting.*

Actions: • Clarify your rights and responsibilities in relation to the dispute.
                • Identify the main issues that need to be discussed and what each party would like to see happen.
                • Get a sense of what each party is prepared to do to get the results, and how the dispute might be resolved if mediation is not successful.

Skill: *Conduct the meeting.*

Actions: • Create a safe environment for each party to talk out their "side" of the dispute privately with you.
                • Set rules for confidentiality.
                • Ask each party to think about what the other party wants.
                • Put yourself in each party's shoes and think about what they expect.
                • Encourage each party to decide how to reach a resolution.

Skill: *Assess satisfaction.*

Actions: • Ask each party how satisfied they are with the outcome of the mediation.
                • Ask what would need to happen to improve their level of satisfaction.

Skill: *Follow up to check on resolution.*

Actions: • Check in with each party a few days after the conclusion of mediation to evaluate the outcome and the current status of the relationship between the parties.
                • Ask yourself, "Is further action required?"

Section 2—Managing for Results

Leadership Competency 76	Managing Meetings
Leadership Competency 77	Managing People
Leadership Competency 78	Managing Projects
Leadership Competency 79	Managing Stress
Leadership Competency 80	Managing Talent
Leadership Competency 81	Managing Quality
Leadership Competency 82	Managing Values and Principles
Leadership Competency 83	Managing Virtual Teams
Leadership Competency 84	Managing the Workforce
Leadership Competency 85	Managing for Health
Leadership Competency 86	Managing for Productivity Improvement
Leadership Competency 87	Managing Time
Leadership Competency 88	Managing the Business
Leadership Competency 89	Managing Careers
Leadership Competency 90	Managing Complexity
Leadership Competency 91	Managing Conflict
Leadership Competency 92	Managing Crises
Leadership Competency 93	Managing Projects and Processes
Leadership Competency 94	Managing Team Performance
Leadership Competency 95	Managing Multicultural Teams
Leadership Competency 96	Managing Individual Performance
Leadership Competency 97	Managing Diversity
Leadership Competency 98	Managing Data
Leadership Competency 99	Managing Information
Leadership Competency 100	Managing Knowledge

Leadership Competency 76:
Managing Meetings

Skill: *Prepare for meetings.*

Actions:
- Ask for meeting input before a meeting so that people can suggest agenda items. Send out the agenda for a meeting at least two days in advance.
- Ask yourself, "How much of this meeting is information sharing, how much is information getting, and how much is problem solving?" Look for ways of balancing sharing, getting, and solving in the meeting.

Skill: *Clarify desired outcomes.*

Actions:
- State your expectations for the meeting.
- Specify what you hope to achieve as a result of the meeting.
- Ask if your image of the desired outcomes matches the participants' image.

(continued)

Leadership Competency 76:
Managing Meetings *(continued)*

Skill:	*Review the agenda.*
Action:	• At the beginning of a meeting, review time frames, topics, presenters, activities, and desired outcomes for each phase of the meeting. Ask participants if the agenda makes sense to them, and whether or not they believe it will accomplish the desired outcomes.

Skill:	*Check on time frames.*
Actions:	• Ask participants if there are any pressing matters that will require them to arrive late, step out during the meeting, or leave early.
	• Ask if the time frames seem reasonable and whether or not the end time is okay with everyone.
	• Ask yourself, "Are there any other meeting limitations or concerns we need to deal with?"

Skill:	*Involve people early in the process.*
Actions:	• Begin the meeting with an activity that allows everyone to speak. Remember the principle: The longer people wait to speak, the less likely they will participate as fully as you want.
	• Ask yourself during the meeting, "Is anyone dominating the discussion? Is there anyone who has not participated at all?"

Skill:	*Respond to input.*
Actions:	• When people contribute their thoughts and feelings, use active listening to clarify their input.
	• Ask yourself, "Do participants seem to believe I am hearing them?"
	• If someone is not talking, consider asking them a question in order to involve them in the discussion (without putting too much pressure on them).

Skill:	*Credit contributions.*
Actions:	• Recognize input by giving credit to people who contribute ideas. For example, you might say, "I like Jane's idea" or "Building on Tom's point . . ."
	• Ask yourself, "Am I letting people know that I appreciate their ideas?"

(continued)

Leadership Competency 76:
Managing Meetings *(concluded)*

Skill: *Manage conflicts.*

Actions:
- Think consciously about strategies to employ when conflicts occur.
- If the relationship is important but the outcome of a discussion is not really important, consider avoiding the conflict or accommodating it.
- If relationship and outcome are of medium importance, then consider ways to compromise.
- If both relationship and outcome are very important, collaborate with the group to find a solution.
- Ask yourself, "Do people feel safe expressing their thoughts, feelings, and disagreements?"

Skill: *Record results and action commitments.*

Actions:
- At the end of the meeting, write down all the decisions that were made and who is responsible for implementing them. Also, summarize next steps for moving forward.
- Ask yourself, "Is everyone clear about the decisions we made and who will be responsible for what commitment?"

Leadership Competency 77:
Managing People

Skill: *Provide fair compensation and benefits.*

Actions: • Analyze compensation based on market comparability and internal equity.
            • Identify gaps between what you pay and what the competition pays for talent.
            • Identify gaps in compensation within your department for people doing similar work.
            • Develop a plan to address the disparities.

Skill: *Provide opportunities to learn and grow.*

Actions: • Encourage people to take advantage of the learning options available.
            • Take an inventory of your options: classroom, self-study, e-learning, Web-based training, knowledge sharing, OJT, Webinars, etc.
            • Set expectations regarding the number of training days per year.

Skill: *Communicate regularly.*

Actions: • Regularly inform your employees about changes.
            • Hold weekly team meetings and quarterly department meetings.
            • Ask yourself, "What could I do to involve people, incorporate people, and inspire people?"

Skill: *Deal with employee relationship problems or issues quickly.*

Actions: • Be open to hearing about problems. Listen to complaints respectfully. Before taking action, do a thorough investigation so that you understand all points of view.
            • Ask yourself, "Do I respond in a timely manner to employee relationship problems?"

Skill: *Manage change effectively.*

Actions: • Describe the desired end state, analyze the current state, and communicate the benefits and advantages of moving from the current state to the desired state for the employee and the organization.
            • Develop learning strategies, reward strategies, and communication strategies.
            • Ask yourself, "Have I sufficiently involved the sponsor, the change agents, and affected group?"
            • Start the change at the top.

Skill: *Conduct effective performance management.*

Actions: • View performance management as a business process.
            • Facilitate alignment, engagement, and growth.
            • Measure contribution and capability development.
            • Use a balanced-scorecard approach.
            • Set clear goals, engage in productive dialogue, and conduct periodic reviews.
            • Connect rewards to performance.

(continued)

Leadership Competency 77:
Managing People *(concluded)*

Skill: *Measure human capital.*

Actions:
- Set goals for turnover of mission-critical talent, the percentage of employees with balanced scorecards, diversity, employee commitment, time to close open requirements, time to develop required skills and capabilities, cost per hire, and cost per training day.
- Review progress on your human capital goals regularly, and develop a "dashboard" to monitor results.
- Ask yourself, "Am I paying as much attention to managing my human capital as I am to managing my finances and customer relationships?"

Leadership Competency 78:
Managing Projects

Skill: *Plan the plan.*

Actions: • Define the scope of your plan.
                • Secure executive support.
                • Identify and develop your team.
                • Conduct a launch meeting to present the plan.

Skill: *Evaluate past projects.*

Actions: • Create a list of past projects that were managed.
                • Analyze what worked and what didn't work on past projects.
                • Establish evaluation criteria.

Skill: *Assess project management.*

Actions: • Create a 5-point scale to assess project management in your organization.
                • Diagnose your current level of effectiveness.
                • Identify your next-level goal and what will be required to meet that goal.
                • Consider integration, scope, time, cost, quality, human resource optimization, communication, and risk management in your scale or scales.

Skill: *Classify projects.*

Actions: • Determine how much management, supervision, and oversight will be required.
                • Estimate the importance of people, culture, process, technology, and knowledge for successful completion.

Skill: *Develop project-management methodologies.*

Actions: • Determine if the project is small, medium, or large, and determine the most appropriate methodology given project size and resources.
                • Define project roles and responsibilities for the sponsor, the manager, the steering committee, and the team.
                • Decide how you will manage risks.

Skill: *Train the staff.*

Actions: • Invite your team to an overview meeting for the project.
                • Conduct a training module for project management methodology.
                • Clarify critical success factors and team requirements.

Skill: *Monitor project-management practices.*

Actions: • Establish clear performance expectations.
                • Conduct regular evaluations and follow-up meetings.
                • Provide coaching (as needed).

Leadership Competency 79: Managing Stress

Skill:	*Recognize stress signals.*
Actions:	• Identify how you react to stress. • Think of how you felt during past or present stressful situations. • Explore how those situations affected your behavior, your physical condition, and your emotions. • Practice tuning in to your *self* to recognize your stress signals at home and at work.

Skill:	*Understand your stressors.*
Actions:	• Look at what's happening in your life and determine the role that events, circumstances, and internal cues play in creating stress. • Ask yourself how frequently the stressor occurs and how much intensity it creates.

Skill:	*Get fit.*
Actions:	• Exercise regularly. • Develop a program that improves your strength, endurance, and flexibility.

Skill:	*Eat right.*
Actions:	• Monitor your diet and its nutritional value. • If you need to lose weight, join Weight Watchers or another support group. • Reduce the fat, caffeine, and refined sugars in your diet.

Skill:	*Relax.*
Actions:	• Learn some basic relaxation techniques, such as deep breathing. • Ask yourself, "How often am I in a state of fight-or-flight?" • Restore balance and harmony in your life.

Skill:	*Reduce interpersonal stress.*
Actions:	• Take a course to improve your interpersonal skills. • Practice listening, observing, and asking questions. • Demonstrate understanding to what others are saying. • Communicate your perspective without using inflammatory content or tone.

Skill:	*Build self-esteem.*
Actions:	• Set realistic expectations. • Focus on the positive. • *Live* who you are. • Replace your self-defeating thoughts with positive self messages.

(continued)

Leadership Competency 79:
Managing Stress *(concluded)*

Skill: *Deal with negative emotions.*

Actions: • Deal with anxiety and depression.
                  • Ask yourself, "Is my level of anxiety or depression interfering with my work?" If so, seek professional help.
                  • Accept ownership of your anger.
                  • Let go of unrealistic expectations.

Leadership Competency 80:
Managing Talent

Skill: *Assess functional and technical capability.*

Actions:
- Identify functional and technical requirements for each job.
- Determine how well the person stacks up against the requirements.
- Identify gaps.

Skill: *Assess culture fit.*

Actions:
- Define desired and required values and norms.
- Determine how congruent the person's values and behaviors are with the stated values and norms.
- Ask yourself, "Will this person thrive in this culture and add value to it?"

Skill: *Assess results of previous experience.*

Actions:
- Review previous job experience.
- Inquire about the results achieved and behaviors used to get those results.
- Ask yourself, "Will this person be able to produce similar or better results in this job?"

Skill: *Assess knowledge, skills, and attitudes.*

Actions:
- Review educational background and life experience.
- Determine the knowledge, skill, and attitude requirements for the job in question.
- Ask yourself, "Does this person have the background and abilities required to be successful in this job?"

Skill: *Assess performance.*

Actions:
- Rate past performance, based on contribution and leadership.
- Ask yourself, "Does this person have a history of exceeding expectations? Is he or she an inspiring force in the organization?"
- Look at both behavior and results when assessing performance.

Skill: *Assess potential.*

Actions:
- Rate potential based on capability and commitment.
- Ask yourself, "Does this person have the knowledge, skills, and experience to do more? And is he or she extremely committed to the organization?"
- Get a sense of how personally accountable this person feels for organizational growth, company growth, and their own professional growth.

Skill: *Reward development and results.*

Actions:
- Recognize efforts to develop.
- Incorporate learning and growth into the performance-management system, and link it to compensation in some meaningful way.
- Link rewards and recognition to results and behaviors.

Leadership Competency 81: Managing Quality

Skill: *Know your customers.*

Actions: • Conduct annual customer satisfaction surveys to determine how well you are satisfying your customers' needs.
                   • Spend time with customers at their sites.
                   • Ask yourself, "When is the last time I went to a customer site to ask how they are doing with our products or services?"

Skill: *Set true customer requirements.*

Actions: • Specify what your customer expects and requires from your products, services, and solutions.
                   • Set relationship goals as well as product goals.
                   • Clarify the requirements you have established with your customer.

Skill: *Concentrate on prevention, not correction.*

Actions: • Don't wait until problems occur before you react. Anticipate problems based on people, process, policy, technology, knowledge, strategy, or cultural issues.
                   • Try to catch and rectify problems as early as possible.

Skill: *Reduce chronic waste.*

Actions: • Measure how much time, money, and materials are wasted due to inefficient processes, technology, etc.
                   • Set goals to reduce waste.
                   • Develop a waste reduction plan, and measure progress.
                   • Ask yourself, "Where is waste occurring, and how much is it costing us?"

Skill: *Pursue a continuous-improvement strategy.*

Actions: • Define the core processes required to run your business efficiently and effectively.
                   • Form teams to explore ways to continuously improve processes and people.
                   • Share the financial results of improvements with the teams.

Skill: *Use a structured methodology for process improvement.*

Actions: • Define the problem.
                   • Identify possible causes.
                   • Evaluate the causes.
                   • Make a change.
                   • Test the change.
                   • Take permanent action—embed the fix into the process for good.

(continued)

Leadership Competency 81:
Managing Quality *(concluded)*

Skill: *Reduce variation.*

Actions: • Use statistical analysis to identify significant variations in cost, time, waste, etc.
                 • Post progress on key measures.
                 • Strive for zero defects.

Skill: *Apply to all functions.*

Actions: • Use TQM in all aspects of the business. Remember, quality is not limited to manufacturing at the individual contributor level.
                 • Apply quality principles (continuous improvement, quality control, quality assurance) to all functions of the business (leadership, marketing, sales, human resources, IT, investor relations, product development, and operations) at all levels.

Leadership Competency 82: Managing Values and Principles

Skill:	*Articulate what's most important to you.*
Actions:	• Go to a Web site on values clarification and answer the questions that will help you to clarify your values. • Check out the company resources on ethics and financial stewardship.

Skill:	*Ask what's most important to others.*
Actions:	• Hold a meeting to explore which values people want and what the organization needs to be successful. • Conduct focus groups to narrow the list of values.

Skill:	*Agree on core values.*
Actions:	• Based on the results of the focus groups, create a cross-functional, multi-level team and ask it to choose five to seven core values and write a behavioral definition for each value. • Send the team's report to the people who participated in the focus groups, and ask for feedback. • Incorporate the feedback and communicate the results.

Skill:	*Perform a values audit on a regular basis.*
Actions:	• Conduct a survey once per year that measures the strength of the core values, the perceived importance of the values, and whether or not the behaviors supporting the values are getting better or getting worse. • Identify gaps between strength and importance. • Form task teams to generate ideas for closing the gaps, strengthening the norms, and aligning the culture.

Skill:	*Know and grow yourself.*
Actions:	• Learn as much about yourself as possible by taking tests and going to courses. • Set your career goals and plans for reaching them. • Decide how you are going to balance work-life issues. • Set priorities. • Engage in appropriate self-disclosure.

(continued)

Leadership Competency 82:
Managing Values and Principles *(concluded)*

Skill: *Know and grow others.*

Actions:
- Take staffing decisions seriously.
- Motivate others by first understanding their values and career objectives.
- Strive to be fair, compassionate, and patient. Listen to people so that you can identify their wants and needs.
- Manage and measure work performance.
- Delegate based on commitment and capability.

Skill: *Know and grow organizational capabilities.*

Actions:
- Understand how the organization works, and strive to be agile in navigating through the corporation.
- Work to improve decision quality and creativity.
- Develop political savvy so that you can choose your initiatives wisely.
- Ask yourself, "Do I have the managerial courage to push for required changes?"
- Drive for results.

Skill: *Know and grow your customers.*

Actions:
- Listen to your customers to understand their needs and opportunities.
- Develop your business acumen so that you can add value and solve their problems.
- Help your customers solve their problems.
- Develop an action orientation so that you can respond quickly to customer needs.
- Ask yourself, "Do I have the functional and technical skills to add value to my customers?"

Leadership Competency 83:
Managing Virtual Teams

Skill:	*Assess team effectiveness.*
Actions:	• Assess commitment, capability, and culture. • Determine the strength, importance, and direction of critical standards of team effectiveness. • Address gaps between importance and effectiveness.

Skill:	*Assess versatility and virtuality.*
Actions:	• Identify the versatile and virtual characteristics of the team that will need to be taken into account in order to be successful. • Determine how many locations, time zones, levels, departments, organizations, and cultures are represented on the team.

Skill:	*Assess stage of development.*
Actions:	• Determine which stage of development the team is in: orientation, trust building, goal clarification, decision making, implementation, high performance, or renewal. • Develop a plan to get to high performance.

Skill:	*Prioritize major issues and opportunities.*
Actions:	• Identify changes and challenges. • Identify make-or-break issues. • Conduct problem-solving sessions to address top priorities.

Skill:	*Develop a common purpose and principles.*
Actions:	• Articulate the vision. • Define the values. • Agree on operating principles and norms.

Skill:	*Establish a plan.*
Actions:	• Define the mission. • Develop goals and objectives.

Skill:	*Define roles and responsibilities.*
Actions:	• Distribute tasks and accountabilities. • Define categories of information that will need to be collected and shared. • Describe the key events facing the team.

(continued)

Leadership Competency 83:
Managing Virtual Teams *(concluded)*

Skill: *Value differences.*

Actions:
- Use an assessment tool to help you understand each person on the team.
- Understand how differences contribute to team effectiveness.
- Develop a plan for leveraging differences.

Skill: *Use interpersonal skills.*

Actions:
- Listen to each other.
- Ask questions.
- Demonstrate understanding.
- Give your perspective.
- Manage conflict.

Skill: *Demonstrate leadership.*

Actions:
- Lead virtually by creating an electronic workspace.
- Facilitate teamwork.
- Manage team communications.

Skill: *Address virtual challenges.*

Action:
- Discuss challenges and strategies related to participation, problem solving, rewards and recognition, learning, communication, and trust.

Leadership Competency 84:
Managing the Workforce

Skill: *Identify business requirements for the future.*

Actions: • Explore market trends.
                • Survey your customers to identify what solutions and relationships they are seeking.
                • Ask yourself, "How will I need to evolve my solutions and relationships to meet customer expectations in the future?"

Skill: *Identify job requirements for the future.*

Actions: • Identify the organizational demands imposed by new customer requirements.
                • Form a discussion group to specify required changes in leadership, marketing, sales, human resources, IT, legal, investor relations, product development, and operations.
                • Translate those organizational requirements into specific job requirements.

Skill: *Identify competency requirements.*

Actions: • Ask yourself, "What new competencies will be required to meet the demands of the jobs in the new organization?"
                • Scale the competencies and identify the required level of proficiency at each job level.

Skill: *Develop a workforce plan.*

Actions: • Assess the current workforce against the requirements for the future.
                • Create a plan that takes into account when new skills will be required and how many people will need to be hired.

Skill: *Identify talent gaps.*

Actions: • Conduct a 360° feedback assessment to determine the gaps between required levels of functioning on the competencies and the current level of functioning.
                • Calculate the gaps for each job at each level.

Skill: *Develop a hiring plan.*

Actions: • Based on the gap analysis and the timeline, create a plan to close the gaps.
                • Use multiple sourcing strategies (e.g., employee referral, Internet recruiting, university recruiting, direct sourcing, and agency sourcing).
                • Ask yourself, "Are we aggressive in our use of recruiting sources?"

(continued)

Leadership Competency 84:
Managing the Workforce *(concluded)*

Skill: *Develop a performance-management system.*

Actions:
- View performance management as a business process.
- Facilitate alignment, engagement, and growth.
- Measure contributions and skill development.
- Use a balanced-scorecard approach.
- Set clear goals, engage in productive dialogue, and conduct periodic reviews.
- Connect rewards to performance.

Leadership Competency 85:
Managing for Health

Skill: *Establish health as a first-priority business need.*

Actions: • Analyze the company's healthcare costs and compare total costs to profits.
                • Estimate the percentage increases in costs if nothing changes.
                • Identify the impacts on people and the business if healthcare costs are not contained.
                • Identify possible solutions for containing healthcare costs and increasing productivity through a healthier workforce.

Skill: *Reinforce the connection between health and productivity.*

Actions: • Identify how your own physical, emotional, and mental health impact your productivity.
                • Encourage employees to recognize how their health impacts their productivity and quality of life.

Skill: *Create a healthy work environment.*

Actions: • Strengthen positive norms in the culture (e.g., respect, involvement, trust, support).
                • Eliminate the negative norms in the culture (e.g., exclusivity, micro-management, self-interest).

Skill: *Assess the impact of management style on health.*

Actions: • Identify how management behaviors impact health.
                • Encourage managers to EMPOWER their employees:
                — **E**mpathize.
                — **M**easure the gap between stated values and actual behaviors.
                — **P**rovide a safe and secure environment.
                — **O**pen up opportunities for learning.
                — **W**in with your employees.
                — **E**ncourage involvement.
                — **R**eward and recognize great performance.

Skill: *Encourage employee wellness.*

Actions: • Have the company join a health promotion program. Incorporate healthy behaviors into the business (e.g., provide healthy alternatives for lunches and breaks, hold meetings while walking, etc.).
                • Reward people who participate in wellness programs.

Leadership Competency 86:
Managing for Productivity Improvement

Skill: *Conduct a survey of your customers.*

Actions:
- Conduct a customer survey to determine the products/services most needed by your customers.
- Identify non-value-added work in your own area and develop an approach to eliminate it (e.g., 1-800 numbers, Web sites, etc.).

Skill: *Develop people.*

Actions:
- Identify competencies required for success.
- Assess people on those competencies.
- Provide opportunities for people to acquire the skills they need to be more productive.
- Make sure people have the support they need to be successful.

Skill: *Articulate strategy.*

Actions:
- Clarify direction by developing and communicating product strategies, market strategies, and distribution strategies.
- In addition, communicate strategies for human capital, information capital, organizational capital, and customer capital.
- Ask yourself, "How clear is the strategic direction to employees at all levels of the organization?"

Skill: *Improve processes.*

Actions:
- Identify the core processes that are critical to the business and that affect productivity.
- Map and analyze the core processes.
- Drive deployment of processes that improve productivity.

Skill: *Invest in technology.*

Actions:
- Ask yourself how your processes could be technology-enabled.
- When building or buying new technology, always consider how to integrate the systems with legacy technology.
- Keep abreast of changes in technology that seem to have the greatest impact on productivity.

Skill: *Align the culture.*

Actions:
- Define and communicate core values.
- Audit those values annually to determine the strength and perceived importance of the stated norms and values.
- Ask yourself, "How well does our culture support our business strategy? Is it an asset or a deficit?"

(continued)

Leadership Competency 86:
Managing for Productivity Improvement (concluded)

Skill: *Manage knowledge.*

Actions: • Define the knowledge requirements for improving productivity.
               • Collect, organize, disseminate, and leverage knowledge from multiple resources.
               • Establish an expert resource network in your organization.
               • Make it easy for people to gain access to the information, knowledge, and wisdom they need for optimal productivity.

Leadership Competency 87: Managing Time

Skill:	*Set goals and priorities.*
Actions:	• Identify your major goals for the year.
	• Group the goals by priority and assign weights to them.
	• Keep these goals and priorities in a visible spot as a constant reminder.

Skill:	*Do a cost analysis of your time.*
Actions:	• Analyze how much time you waste on unnecessary tasks.
	• Assign a cost value to that time.

Skill:	*Keep activity logs.*
Actions:	• Keep track of all of your activities for a week.
	• Ask yourself, "How well do these activities align with my goals and priorities?"
	• Identify the non-aligned activities you can stop doing.

Skill:	*Develop action plans.*
Actions:	• Refer to your goals and develop objectives and tasks required to achieve them.
	• Create a timeline that shows which tasks will need to be completed each month to achieve your quarterly objectives.
	• Estimate the time required to do each task.

Skill:	*Create to-do lists.*
Actions:	• Review your objectives and tasks, and create daily "to-do" lists that support those tasks.
	• Start each day with a list of critical "to-do" steps.
	• Review the list at the end of each day, and check off those steps you accomplished.

Skill:	*Develop planning and scheduling skills.*
Actions:	• Learn a planning methodology that enables you to have visibility to your vision, mission, goals, objectives, tasks, and strategies.
	• Purchase a PDA to help you with your scheduling.
	• Learn Microsoft Outlook or a similar software program so that you can make scheduling throughout the organization more efficient.

(continued)

Leadership Competency 87:
Managing Time *(concluded)*

Skill: *Delegate specific projects and activities to your team.*

Actions:
- Assign work to your team that you don't need to do yourself.
- Ask yourself, "Am I being too controlling? And am I trying to do too much myself?"
- When you delegate work, always assess the commitment and capability of your team to do the work successfully.

Skill: *Improve decision-making skills.*

Actions:
- Acquire the fundamental principles of decision making:
  1. Define the criteria or objectives.
  2. Expand the list of alternatives.
  3. Weight the objectives.
  4. Seek out sufficient decision information.
  5. Compare alternatives.
  6. Choose the alternative that satisfies the most important criteria or objectives.
- Ask yourself, "Do I have the ability to make timely and accurate decisions?"

Leadership Competency 88:
Managing the Business

Skill: *Manage people.*

Actions:
- Assess the talent in your organization. Determine how many detractors, observers, participants, contributors, and leaders you have in your organization.
- Distribute work according to commitment and capability.
- Recognize that human capital is your most important asset.

Skill: *Manage processes.*

Actions:
- Identify the core processes in your work.
- Analyze the processes to make sure there is a smooth, efficient, and effective work flow.
- Re-engineer processes for continuous improvement.
- Conduct process mapping to make sure everyone understands interdependencies and decision points.

Skill: *Manage policies.*

Actions:
- Review your policies on an annual basis.
- Make sure the policies continue to reflect current conditions and standards.
- Ask yourself, "Are my policies functional and not overly burdensome or bureaucratic?"

Skill: *Manage projects.*

Actions:
- Set goals, timelines, milestones, and deliverables.
- Monitor progress on all milestones. If there is a significant variance between the "plan" and the "actual," conduct a review to determine root causes.
- Identify corrective action based on the root causes.

Skill: *Manage technology.*

Actions:
- Stay current on changes in technology.
- Review technologies that could enable and/or accelerate your performance.
- If you buy or build new technology, always ask first what impact the new technology will have on legacy systems.
- Ask yourself, "What can we do to build an integrated and effective system?"

(continued)

Leadership Competency 88:
Managing the Business *(concluded)*

Skill: *Manage knowledge.*

Actions: • Define the knowledge requirements you have for your work and projects.
            • Develop a system to collect and capture information and knowledge that will help on an ongoing basis.
            • Decide on categories for organizing the knowledge to make it more accessible and usable.
            • Determine how you will distribute and disseminate the knowledge.
            • Always encourage people to leverage the knowledge base to solve business and customer problems.

Skill: *Manage organizational culture.*

Actions: • Decide on the norms and values your organization will need to institutionalize to be successful.
            • Involve a broad and representative set of employees to identify the desired and required norms and values.
            • After you have articulated and communicated the values, conduct an annual culture audit to measure the strength of the values.
            • Ask yourself, "Is cultural alignment a key business priority for me?"

Skill: *Manage finances.*

Actions: • Establish clear revenue and expense goals.
            • Monitor progress on these goals relentlessly.
            • Communicate to your organization not only the importance of meeting financial goals, but also your expectation that every person manages company funds like they would manage their own.

Leadership Competency 89: Managing Careers

Skill: *Identify a career objective.*

Actions:
- Reflect on what you have liked and disliked in your career.
- Ask yourself why you liked or disliked different jobs.
- Write a short-term and a long-term career objective.

Skill: *Define your values.*

Actions:
- Explore the factors in previous jobs or life experiences that gave you a sense of satisfaction and meaning.
- Write down all the values that contributed to satisfaction and meaning.
- Organize the values into physical values (for example, salary, travel, or location), emotional values (for example, respect, teamwork, interpersonal relationships), intellectual values (for example, variety, challenge, and learning), and spiritual values (for example, connectedness, community, or contribution).

Skill: *Create a résumé.*

Actions:
- State your job objective upfront.
- Summarize your work and life experience.
- List the jobs you have had, starting from the most recent.
- Briefly describe the job and list the specific contributions and results you achieved in that job.
- List your educational experience, certifications, and publications.
- Make sure you include complete contact information.
- Decide whether or not you want to provide references or indicate that you will provide references upon request.
- Be brief and powerful.
- Keep your résumé to less than two pages.

Skill: *Define your competitive edge.*

Actions:
- Identify your core competencies.
- Think about your special characteristics and the ways in which you are different from others.
- Write down your unique talents, experiences, skills, education, and results.
- Don't be afraid to state clearly your competitive edge, but don't inflate your résumé in any way.

(continued)

Leadership Competency 89:
Managing Careers (*concluded*)

Skill: *Hone your interviewing skills.*

Actions:
- Prepare in advance for the interview.
- Find out as much as you can about the company and the person who will be interviewing you.
- Do a practice interview with a trusted friend.
- Prepare an opening statement that summarizes your experience.
- Keep it short.
- Clarify questions the interviewer asks before you answer them.
- Come with a list of questions you have about the company and the job.
- Stay calm, collected, and confident.
- Position your body so that you are square to the interviewer. Lean slightly forward to signal interest and attentiveness.
- Resist engaging in distracting behavior, such as tapping your foot or picking at your nails.

Skill: *Develop good references.*

Actions:
- Remember: Career management is about developing relationships and performing.
- It is about results and behavior.
- Ask people if they will serve as your references.
- Tell them the points you want them to emphasize.

Skill: *Conduct a thorough search of possibilities.*

Actions:
- Find out more about all possible jobs and careers that interest you.
- Be expansive.
- Ask others what careers they think you would excel in.
- Refer to the dictionary of occupational titles to build your list.

Skill: *Compare alternatives according to values.*

Actions:
- Create a grid; list all viable job alternatives across the horizontal axis on the top and list your values down the vertical axis.
- Rank your values from most-important to least-important.
- Ask yourself for each job alternative, "How well does this job satisfy this value?"
- When you complete each cell in the grid, see which job has the most pluses.

Leadership Competency 90:
Managing Complexity

Skill: *Encourage and assist interdisciplinary research.*

Actions:
- Join groups that are engaged in interdisciplinary research.
- Practice looking at problems from multiple points of view.
- Encourage your colleagues to explore multiple sources of input before coming to solutions.

Skill: *Explore collaboratively.*

Actions:
- Ask yourself, "Am I engaging enough people in this exploration?"
- Ask your colleagues for their input.
- Seek out different points of view on problems.
- Ask yourself, "Am I judging input too quickly? Or am I staying open to new ideas?"
- Don't express your point of view during the collaboration phase.

Skill: *Search for patterns.*

Actions:
- Identify common themes in what you are studying.
- Look for ideas that seem to repeat themselves.
- Analyze social networks and see how the pattern of relationships form and build.

Skill: *Create imaginative and robust models.*

Actions:
- Free yourself to look at problems in innovative ways.
- Search the Internet for new models to apply to the complex problems you are trying to solve.
- Ask yourself, "Am I generating lists, or am I framing the problem in multi-dimensional ways?"

Skill: *Use computer simulations.*

Actions:
- Practice computer games that solve complex problems.
- Apply the learning from those games to a problem at work.

Skill: *Promote and try out theoretical and practical applications.*

Actions:
- Inquire about the theory of "complexity science."
- Go to the Internet and do a search on complexity.
- Read a book on complexity science.

(continued)

Leadership Competency 90:
Managing Complexity *(concluded)*

Skill: *Think multi-dimensionally.*

Actions:
- Try framing problems two-dimensionally, instead of thinking linearly or developing lists.
- Ask yourself, "What are the functions, processes, and components I am dealing with?" If you can answer those questions, you can frame a problem by taking any two sets of answers.
- Create a two-dimensional grid that represents the processes and functions for a problem you are trying to solve.

Leadership Competency 91: Managing Conflict

Skill:	*Identify the conflict.*
Actions:	• Write down a list of conflicts you are facing at home and at work. • Describe the nature of the conflict. • Rate each conflict on a scale of 1 to 5 (1 = *minimal discomfort* and 5 = *major angst*).

Skill:	*Rate the level of satisfaction each party has with the current situation.*
Actions:	• Think about the other party's situation and concerns. • Ask yourself, "How satisfied are they with the current status?" • Ask yourself the same question. • Rate the level of current satisfaction for both parties on a scale of 1 to 5 (1 = *low* and 5 = *high*).

Skill:	*Assess how important the relationship is to you.*
Actions:	• Consider how much this relationship means to you. • Ask yourself, "Is this a relationship in which I will be involved for an extended period of time?" • Decide if this is a relationship in which you want to invest time and energy.

Skill:	*Assess how important the outcome is to you.*
Actions:	• Determine how important it is to you to achieve a particular outcome. • Ask yourself, "Is the outcome of this conflict worth an investment of time and energy?" • Decide how much you want to invest in achieving the outcome.

Skill:	*Seek to understand the other person's point of view.*
Actions:	• Reflect upon the other person's point of view. Inquire about what's important to them in this conflict. • Assess how important the relationship and outcome are to them.

(continued)

Leadership Competency 91:
Managing Conflict *(concluded)*

Skill: *Choose the strategy that will give you the desired level of relationship and outcome.*

Actions: • If the relationship is important and the outcome is not that important, think about avoiding the conflict or accommodating the other person.
                  • If the relationship and the outcome are of medium importance to you, then think about a compromise strategy.
                  • If the relationship is not important and the outcome is important, think about the best ways to compete and win, even if it means that the other person loses.
                  • If both the relationship and outcome are important, then think about ways to collaborate with the person so that both of you can achieve a high level of satisfaction from the outcome.

Skill: *Improve performance through conflict.*

Actions: • Look at conflict as a way to elevate your performance and the performance of your team.
                  • Identify different points of view, and learn from them.
                  • Seek to collaborate on problems, even if it means investing more time and energy.
                  • Ask yourself, "How could a collaborative approach help me achieve my relationship goals as well as my outcome goals?"

Leadership Competency 92: Managing Crises

Skill:	*Forecast potential crises.*
Actions:	• Try to anticipate possible sources of disruption.
	• Expand your list by adding the following disruption categories: political, economic, competitive, loss of key people, terrorist activity.
	• Put together a crisis management team that can mobilize if any forecasted event occurs.

Skill:	*Communicate carefully.*
Actions:	• If a crisis should occur, manage the communication thoughtfully.
	• Be careful not to use inflammatory language.
	• Ask yourself, "Am I holding myself to the highest standards of accuracy and rationality?" Remember: In a crisis, people are desperate for calm, clear, straightforward messages that communicate your concern for them.

Skill:	*Maintain positive relationships with stakeholders.*
Actions:	• Go out of your way to make contact with key stakeholders in a crisis.
	• Involve them as your thinking partners.
	• Ask yourself, "Have I involved the right people in my thinking?"

Skill:	*Prepare for confrontational interviews.*
Actions:	• Anticipate confrontations that may come from any source.
	• List the hard questions you may be asked. Write down your responses to those questions.
	• Practice your responses with a colleague before you conduct the interview.

Skill:	*Identify your vulnerabilities.*
Actions:	• Be honest and open with yourself about your weaknesses and vulnerabilities.
	• Decide which of the vulnerabilities you can and should share. Remember, acknowledging the vulnerabilities you can share increases your credibility and the probability that people will hear the message you are trying to send.
	• Ask yourself, "Will sharing this vulnerability help or hurt the situation?"

Skill:	*Establish policies and procedures for emergency response.*
Actions:	• Assemble a team, and write procedures in advance of a crisis if possible. In a time of crisis, it is hard to think clearly. Thus, policies and procedures will help you navigate the crisis rationally.
	• Ask yourself, "What policies and procedures do we have in place now, should there be a crisis?"

(continued)

Leadership Competency 92:
Managing Crises (concluded)

Skill:	*Coordinate outreach efforts.*
Actions:	• Develop clear and consistent messages during a crisis.
	• Try to avoid conflicting communications.
	• Ask yourself, "Who might be reaching out during this crisis?"
	• Bring everyone together and coordinate your efforts.

Skill:	*Reduce risks of business losses and human suffering.*
Action:	• Always keep in mind the risks to the business and to the people. Identify the possible risks, and put together a plan for mitigating them.

Leadership Competency 93:
Managing Projects and Processes

Skill: *Analyze and prioritize your work priorities.*

Actions:
- Analyze your work on a weekly basis and determine your priorities for the week. Then, on a daily basis, plan in detail the work you want to complete that day.
- Allow time each day for planning and thinking. Plan tomorrow's activities at the end of each day.

Skill: *Develop methods for keeping track of your work and promises.*

Actions:
- Begin establishing methods for keeping track of your work and your promises (e.g., set personal deadlines, record due dates and appointments in a time management calendar, etc.).
- Develop measurements that track achievements vs. initial goals.

Skill: *Use project-management software.*

Actions:
- Use project-management software (such as Microsoft Project) to develop project plans, commitments, deliverables, timelines, etc.
- When possible, use collaborative software so that your team members can share project data, schedules, etc.

Skill: *Use time-management principles to accomplish tasks in less time.*

Actions:
- Keep meetings on schedule by using time limits and ground rules. Develop, disseminate, use agendas for meetings, conferences, and presentations.
- Use a scheduling calendar/day timer, and plan follow-up activities.

Leadership Competency 94:
Managing Team Performance

Skill:	*Include a team-performance appraisal as part of the performance-management system.*
Action:	• Use an appraisal of team performance in addition to appraisal of individual performance as a part of your performance-management system.

Skill:	*Coach or participate in teams outside work.*
Actions:	• Coach or participate in teams outside work (e.g., political, community service, sports teams). • Identify the specific behaviors that lead to great results in different types of teams.

Skill:	*Facilitate a brainstorming session.*
Actions:	• Facilitate a brainstorming session, a training session with breakout groups, or a process improvement session. • Identify the ideas that have the most potential for improving performance. • Assign a team to implement those ideas, and ask the team to report back on progress.

Skill:	*Gain exposure to a major business issue or initiative.*
Actions:	• Perform in a role that exposes you to a major business change initiative or issue (e.g., a new system, a major development effort, an organizational start-up, or a major reorganization). • Identify the specific skills and behaviors that lead to positive results. • Try to apply those skills and behaviors to your own team.

Skill:	*Lead a large project with multiple teams.*
Actions:	• Lead a large project that includes formation of multiple but integrated teams, where you must clarify and facilitate the performance of responsibilities with team leaders and negotiate and coordinate significant resources. • Lead an organization that supports one or more businesses that engages in such activities as establishing effective communication with the business teams, developing methodologies and procedures, or creating a positive internal and external team environment.

Skill:	*Lead an effort that involves a major structural realignment.*
Actions:	• Lead an effort that involves a major structural realignment (e.g., start-up, significant growth, downsizing, plant closing, restructuring, business turnaround, acquisition, or partnership). • Set specific goals, and review progress on those goals with the team.

(continued)

Leadership Competency 94:
Managing Team Performance *(concluded)*

Skill: *Manage a diverse project team.*

Actions:
- Manage a project team of diverse members who have different levels of experience than you.
- Identify behaviors that worked for a different team but that don't work as well in this team.

Skill: *Set up regular review meetings to keep projects on track.*

Actions:
- When leading a large project that involves other functions, set up regular review meetings to ensure that things are on track.
- Ask for feedback on which behaviors led to the best results.

Skill: *Take on a role in a cross-functional business team outside of your area.*

Actions:
- Observe and participate in a team meeting from another function.
- Identify the behaviors that seem to lead to the best performance results.

Leadership Competency 95:
Managing Multicultural Teams

Skill: *Create an environment of respect for differences.*

Actions:
- Support an atmosphere where people of all backgrounds are valued and where it is safe for all employees to ask for support or information.
- Actively seek information and input from people with varying backgrounds. Include them in decision making and problem solving.
- Challenge any displays of intolerance from others. This should be done privately, but in all cases, you must address intolerant and disrespectful behavior.

Skill: *Increase your sensitivity to issues of diversity.*

Actions:
- Over the period of a few weeks, monitor the assumptions you make about people and ideas.
- Recognize the ways in which your assumptions affect the way you see/experience/value people and ideas that differ from your own.
- Ask yourself if the assumptions you are making about a person's background are getting in the way of understanding or seeing the person as an individual, instead of as a representative of a group.

Skill: *Assess your beliefs about valuing diversity.*

Actions:
- Assess your own attitudes, assumptions, and feelings about people who are different from you.
- Ask yourself what assumptions you make about others that are based on external, easily identifiable differences, as well as more subtle, invisible ones.
- Challenge yourself to acknowledge the assumptions you have about people who are different from you, and the way this affects how you view, develop perceptions of, and treat others.

Skill: *Recruit and promote for workforce diversity.*

Actions:
- Develop specific strategies to increase the flow of applicants and employees from varying backgrounds.
- Make sure that the recruiting pool itself represents a diversity of backgrounds. Are you advertising in the same places/venues or recruiting from only certain colleges? What ways could you broaden your scope to target people from different backgrounds?
- Study other companies or even other units to see what they are doing to recruit and develop multicultural teams. Be willing to hire people with nontraditional backgrounds and skills. Implement support systems to get them up to speed quickly so that they feel part of the team.

(continued)

Leadership Competency 95:
Managing Multicultural Teams *(concluded)*

Skill: *Help people from diverse backgrounds succeed.*

Actions:
- Make sure employees understand the "unwritten" as well as the written rules of the organization and how to work with them or around them where necessary.
- Assign employees from diverse backgrounds to cross-organizational teams and task forces, increasing their exposure to employees from other divisions and departments.
- Recognize and confront aspects of your organizational culture that prevent capable employees who represent other cultures from being fully included and finding success within your organization.

Skill: *Examine and discuss your own background.*

Actions:
- Explore your identity by thinking of all the groups with which you identify.
- Draw a circle and assign different size "slices" to the pie according to the different group identities you have. Some "slices" may be larger than others because they have more significance.
- Use this exercise as a way to examine your own background and the different "identities" you have. Compare your findings with those of your co-workers and discuss the implications of your similarities and differences. What are the advantages and challenges?

Leadership Competency 96:
Managing Individual Performance

Skill: *Link individual and team goals to organizational priorities.*

Actions: • Start with the corporate and organizational objectives.
                • At the beginning of the year, cascade goals throughout the organization.

Skill: *Clarify expectations.*

Actions: • Ask employees to set their individual goals in relation to the corporate
                  and organizational goals.
                • Meet with individual employees to make sure you and the employee
                  have the same image of what's expected.
                • Review individual goals and objectives to ensure that they are specific,
                  measurable, achievable, ratable, and time-bound.

Skill: *Make sure employees understand how their work contributes to the overall
                success of the organization.*

Actions: • Ask individual employees to discuss how their work contributes to the
                  organization's vision, mission, and values.
                • Give your perspective on the importance of their work.

Skill: *Use a system for planning, communicating, and revising priorities.*

Actions: • Schedule dates for setting goals, reviewing progress, and evaluating
                  performance.
                • Ask yourself how frequently you need to meet with each employee to
                  make sure the employee achieves the required results.
                • Be open to changing priorities based on changing conditions.

Skill: *Create contribution goals.*

Actions: • Use a balanced scorecard for measuring performance. Include measures
                  such as financial contribution, customer focus, internal business process,
                  learning, and growth.
                • Clarify how each contribution is weighted and how performance will be
                  rewarded.

Skill: *Create capability development plans.*

Actions: • Identify the competencies required for current job goals and future
                  business needs.
                • Discuss with the employee what knowledge, skills, abilities, behaviors,
                  and attitudes are required for success.
                • Discuss with the employee his/her strengths and weaknesses on each
                  and ask him/her to create a development plan.

(continued)

Leadership Competency 96:
Managing Individual Performance *(concluded)*

Skill: *Provide constructive feedback on contribution and capability development.*

Actions:
- During the year, meet with the employee to discuss progress on all dimensions of the balanced scorecard.
- Engage the employee in discussions about strategic direction.
- Recognize positive performance.
- Encourage the employee to continue to work on their skill-development plan.

Skill: *Conduct an annual performance review.*

Actions:
- Evaluate specific, observable, and job-related behavior only.
- Identify areas needing improvement.
- Recognize positive performance.
- Evaluate the entire year evenly. Don't surprise the employee with critical feedback that he or she is hearing for the first time in the annual review. Practice giving feedback that is specific and behavioral.
- When the person achieves a goal or completes work, make sure to give positive feedback to reinforce the behavior (avoid feedback that is personalized or judgmental).

Skill: *Develop performance management systems that support business strategies.*

Action:
- Develop performance management systems that support your business strategies and goals (e.g., analyze current systems and make recommendations).

Skill: *Provide ongoing feedback and development tips to team members.*

Actions:
- Use 360° assessments as a way to provide developmental advice to your team. Provide expert coaching (i.e., an outside consultant) to each individual.
- Seek out other role models for good coaching and consulting skills.
- Watch them in action or work together on a project to learn their techniques.

Leadership Competency 97:
Managing Diversity

Skill:	*Create a diversity steering committee.*
Action:	• Establish a multicultural and cross-functional group to oversee diversity initiatives in your organization. Identify ways to leverage diversity.

Skill:	*Base promotions on performance.*
Actions:	• Base promotions on merit rather than relationship.
	• Create a fair playing field for all members of the organization.

Skill:	*Build a business case for diversity.*
Actions:	• Conduct research on the business benefits of diversity.
	• Communicate the results of the business case.
	• Use the facts to strengthen diversity efforts and commitment.

Skill:	*Create a culture of respect and inclusiveness.*
Actions:	• Inculcate norms that define respect ("We value differences; we treat everyone as unique individuals; and we give people a sense of dignity and worth.").
	• Ingrain norms that define inclusiveness ("We are open; we are inviting; we share power; and we welcome differences.").

Skill:	*Establish a mentoring program.*
Actions:	• Give minority members of the community access to high-powered mentors in the organization who will advocate for them and provide learning and access opportunities.
	• Train mentors in mentoring skills.

Skill:	*Offer diversity training.*
Action:	• Provide classroom and e-learning training. Start at the top, and bring the program into all areas of the organization.

Skill:	*Tap diverse sourcing pools.*
Actions:	• Review your most frequently used sourcing pools.
	• Identify what percentage of new hires comes from employee referrals, Internet recruiting, agencies, and direct sourcing.
	• Expand your sourcing options to include organizations that represent minority groups and women.

(continued)

Leadership Competency 97:
Managing Diversity *(concluded)*

Skill: *Leverage diversity.*

Actions:
- See differences as gifts.
- Determine workforce differences in style, experience, and cultural perspective.
- Identify and try to understand the introverts and extroverts, the diplomats and the take-charge people, the big-picture and the detail people, and the people who like to keep things open and the people who like to close issues.
- Strive to understand these differences, and use them in decision making and problem solving.

Skill: *Encourage people to become competent in intercultural communication.*

Actions:
- Ask colleagues to participate in cross-cultural groups.
- Involve colleagues in meetings in which there are representatives from multiple ethnic or cultural backgrounds. If possible, take a colleague with you when doing business internationally.

Skill: *Strengthen diversity initiatives.*

Actions:
- Participate in a diversity training session.
- If you are recruiting for a new hire, make sure that you tap into sources of recruits representing other cultures and minority groups.
- Mentor a person from a different ethnic group than your own.

Skill: *Manage workplace diversity.*

Actions:
- Be sensitive to differences in culture.
- Think inclusively.
- Ask yourself, "Am I respecting and making the most of differences among my colleagues?"

Skill: *Reduce barriers to multi-culturalism.*

Actions:
- Review and eliminate policies that give preferential treatment to white males (e.g., golf club memberships). Recognize and promote the understanding that multiculturalism is a fundamental characteristic of organizational life.
- Promote the full and equitable participation of individuals and communities of all origins in shaping the organization's culture.

Leadership Competency 98:
Managing Data

Skill: *Analyze data.*

Action: • Learn how to do t-tests, analysis of variance, and regression analysis. At a minimum, become aware of these processes by purchasing books and/or statistical study guides.

Skill: *Build and manage data repositories.*

Actions: • Link your data to your core business processes.
                 • Be sure to understand where data inputs and outputs belong in the context of your business process.

Skill: *Create databases.*

Actions: • Develop report formats.
                 • Import and clean the data.

Skill: *Use spreadsheet programs.*

Actions: • Learn how to use Excel's built-in statistics calculations.
                 • Use report tables, charts, and graphs to illustrate results.

Skill: *Manage compliance standards.*

Actions: • Tighten requirements concerning data privacy, network security, and intellectual property rights.
                 • Act to prevent data misuse, identity theft, and hacking.

Leadership Competency 99: Managing Information

Skill: *Fortify network security.*

Actions:
- Adopt a sender-authentication scheme.
- Improve access control and identity management.

Skill: *Integrate the enterprise.*

Actions:
- Plan and implement systems that will help employees, customers, clients, and partners turn company knowledge into profit.
- Get essential information on internal portal integration, data integration, standards, and supply chain management.

Skill: *Maximize investments in information technology.*

Actions:
- Accept large installations in phases, and negotiate specific warranties.
- Expect vendors to provide a standard set of warranties.
- Get essential information on measuring ROI, asset management, and total cost of ownership.

Skill: *Align information technology and business goals.*

Actions:
- Seek first to understand the business.
- Establish IT as a driver of business success.
- Get essential information on communicating corporate goals, driving business transformation, and assisting the strategic planning process.

Skill: *Empower a mobile workforce.*

Actions:
- Free your organization from the limitations of cables, desktops, and offices without wasting money on leading-edge technology that will never pay for itself.
- Keep current on fast-paced developments in wireless standards, wireless security, and mobile application development.

Skill: *Optimize the infrastructure.*

Actions:
- Make discriminating choices about PCs; thin client-servers, portables, and desktops.
- Learn about the latest solutions and analyses regarding OS migration initiatives, wiring and environmental concerns, disaster recovery planning, grid computing, and voice-over IP.

Leadership Competency 100:
Managing Knowledge

Skill:	*Define knowledge requirements.*
Actions:	• Identify who will use the information. • Specify what information is needed. • Determine how and when the information will be used. • Specify where the information will come from—the information source.

Skill:	*Capture information.*
Actions:	• Anticipate how the information will be organized. • Collect the input. • Clean the input. • Convert the input to information. • Control the quality of the information.

Skill:	*Organize information.*
Actions:	• Capture information in the format and form that is most comfortable to the source of the input. • Reorganize the information to meet the needs of the user. • Develop procedures for storing, coding, linking, testing, and keeping the information current.

Skill:	*Distribute information.*
Actions:	• Sort out what kind of information you need to disseminate—explicit or tacit. • Select the right tools to disseminate the information. • Determine how the information will be prepared, moved, and received. • Decide how the information will be made available, when it will be available, who will make it available, what format it will be available in, what tool will be used, and who will provide troubleshooting support.

Skill:	*Leverage knowledge.*
Actions:	• Decide how the information will be used. Identify obstacles to receiving and using the information. • Hold debriefing sessions after each major project or sales opportunity to understand how knowledge could have been used more successfully. • Ask yourself, "How useful is the knowledge that we are using?"

Section 3—Achieving Profitability

Leadership Competency 101:
Driving Accountability

Skill: *Establish clear standards and performance expectations.*

Action:
- Establish clear standards and performance expectations with team members for yourself and others. When standards and expectations are clear, everyone will know what is expected, when it is due, and how it will be measured.

Skill: *Perform reality checks with other team members about completing tasks.*

Actions:
- Do a reality check with your team about the tasks you are planning to complete.
- Use the 5WH method: **W**ho is doing **w**hat? **W**here and **w**hen is the work supposed to de done? **W**hy is the work important? **H**ow will results be measured?
- Be sure to record decisions and plans.

Skill: *Solicit feedback about the impact of your activities on others.*

Actions:
- Actively solicit information regarding how your activities and projects are impacting others (positively and negatively).
- Ask how your behaviors are affecting how other people's work gets done and how it is making them feel.

Skill: *Start delegating more activities to team members.*

Action:
- Delegation depends on the commitment and capabilities of the person to whom the work is being delegated, as well as the organization's support for the work. Based on the levels of commitment, capability, and cultural support, decide how much direction, support, and coaching will be needed to make the activity successful.

(continued)

Leadership Competency 101:
Driving Accountability *(concluded)*

Skill: *Summarize your commitments with customers or colleagues.*

Action: • After a meeting with a customer or colleague, summarize your commitments in writing and provide them with a follow-up copy or e-mail.

Skill: *Conduct regular performance reviews.*

Actions: • Set specific objectives for yourself and for others.
• Review progress on those objectives at least once per quarter, but preferably once per month.
• Hold yourself and others accountable for the commitment made and documented.

Skill: *Use team members to assess changes/delays to projects.*

Action: • When project delays or problems occur that affect others, call together all members to assess priorities, re-assign roles, and gain buy-in for a new game plan.

Leadership Competency 102: Driving Profitability

Skill: *Increase revenue.*

Actions:
- Always look for new sales opportunities.
- Cross-sell existing accounts, expand new accounts, and continually explore new markets and product opportunities.
- Protect your base and generate new business.

Skill: *Manage expenses.*

Actions:
- Create a budget with line items for every possible expense category.
- Project month-by-month expenditures, using rigorous analysis and conservative assumptions.

Skill: *Manage the budget.*

Actions:
- Monitor budget-to-actual variances on a monthly basis.
- Relentlessly investigate overages.
- Communicate clearly your expectations that every person on the team will manage his or her budget, and that everyone must treat the company money as if it were their own.

Skill: *Report results.*

Actions:
- Track progress and tell the team which areas you are below budget on and which areas you are over budget on. Identify the reasons why you are above or below your budget numbers.
- Ask yourself, "Does my boss know where we stand with our budget, and the reasons for any variances?"

Leadership Competency 103:
Aligning the Culture

Skill: *Define core values.*

Actions: • Generate a list of values by asking team members what is most important to them and to the business regarding how we do our work.
               • Narrow the list by asking each person to pick the top five values from the expanded list.
               • Choose the five to seven most important values for operating the business.
               • Ask yourself, "Which values are desired and required to optimize working conditions and to implement the strategy?"
               • Write definitions for each of the core values.

Skill: *Define supporting norms.*

Actions: • Ask yourself, "What behaviors would I see if this value existed in our culture?"
               • Write three to five norms for each value. Use this format: Around here we . . . For example, if respect is a core value, then you might write, "Around here we value differences."

Skill: *Diagnose the current state.*

Actions: • After you have defined the desired and required values and norms, conduct a survey to see how people in the organization believe the organization is doing on those values and norms.
               • For each norm, ask people to rate on a 1–5 scale how strong each norm currently is, how important the norm is, and in which direction it is moving (Is it getting better? Or is it getting worse?).

Skill: *Develop people and programs.*

Actions: • Based on the results of the culture audit, identify ways to develop people in order to close the gaps.
               • Also develop a learning strategy, a communications strategy, and a rewards strategy for aligning the culture.

Skill: *Deliver skills and support.*

Actions: • After you have developed your strategies, put together an implementation plan to align the culture.
               • Ask yourself, "Do we have the skills and support we need to be successful with this change?"

Skill: *Determine results.*

Actions: • On an annual basis, take a culture audit to determine progress at closing the gaps and aligning the culture.
               • Share the results with the whole organization.
               • Form task teams to continue improvements in these areas.

Leadership Competency 104:
Re-Engineering Processes

Skill:	*Select the right process to re-engineer.*
Actions:	• Expand the list of processes that are used in your department. • Ask yourself, "Which of these processes are core to the business?" • Select the most critical process that has the biggest impact on the business.

Skill:	*Identify team members and responsibilities.*
Actions:	• Involve a cross-functional team in the project to re-design a process or create a process map. • Invite team members who are affected directly or indirectly by the process. Clarify expectations and timelines.

Skill:	*Re-engineer the process.*
Actions:	• Make the work more understandable by making a flowchart. • Identify where decisions are made, and make sure there is clear authority for the decisions. • Illustrate the sequence of events and how work flows.

Skill:	*Analyze the process.*
Actions:	• Review the map and identify bottlenecks, sources of delay, errors being fixed vs. prevented, role ambiguity, duplications, unnecessary steps, and cycle time. • Change the process map to address any problems identified.

Skill:	*Identify measures of success.*
Actions:	• Consider metrics in the areas of customer satisfaction, organizational performance, supplier satisfaction, financial improvement, and employee satisfaction. • Choose metrics for which accurate and complete data are available, that don't cause people to act in ways that are contrary to the business, and that are simple and SMART. • Ask yourself, "Are these measures driving us to do the right thing?"

Skill:	*Document and deploy the "to-be" process.*
Actions:	• After you have mapped and analyzed the process, develop an implementation plan. • Review progress on the plan at regular intervals. • Ask yourself, "How are we doing on our measures of success?"

Leadership Competency 105:
Focusing on the Customer

Skill: *Conduct focus groups with potential customers.*

Actions:
- Conduct focus groups with potential customers who do not use your products or services.
- Determine why they don't do business with you and what you can do to win their business.
- Use the process, "Get, Give, Merge, Go." **Get** their understanding of your value. **Give** them your ideas about how they can benefit from your company. **Merge** the two "images" to reflect their needs and your ability to meet and exceed their needs. Then **go** with at least one action step that involves further contact.

Skill: *Conduct interviews with key customers to determine how they view your relationship.*

Actions:
- Conduct in-depth interviews with key customers to determine how they view your relationship (its strengths and its weaknesses). What do they think the focus of your relationship should be in the year ahead?
- Have each customer state specifically one thing they would like you to start doing, one thing they would like you to stop doing, and the most important thing they want you to continue doing.

Skill: *Create a monthly newsletter for internal communication.*

Action:
- Create a monthly internal newsletter that includes tips on dealing with customer requests and complaints, customer-focused policies and procedures, summaries of current customer-service readings, and recognition of excellent customer service.

Skill: *Define your company's global market to match products to needs.*

Actions:
- Define your company's global market—the countries where your company presently does business or would like to do business.
- Determine how your company's products can meet the needs of the people in those countries.
- Assess your company's readiness by rating the economic impact and the likelihood of success on a scale of 1 to 5.

Skill: *Develop a customer service survey.*

Actions:
- Develop a customer-service survey to obtain feedback for improving service.
- Ask for feedback on the effectiveness and importance of your services, and whether or not your services are getting better or getting worse from their point of view.
- On the survey, list five value statements. Ask respondents to rate each statement (1 to 5) by agreement, importance, and trend (getting better or worse).

(continued)

Leadership Competency 105:
Focusing on the Customer *(continued)*

Skill: *Develop profiles of key accounts.*

Actions:
- Develop profiles of all key accounts, and include such information as the names of key contacts, office hours, possible new contacts (use a Web-based tracking system to profile accounts—such as Salesforce.com).
- Rate each account according to two variables. First, is the status of the relationship growing or deteriorating? Second, is there potential for new business this quarter and this year?

Skill: *Develop standards for products/services that meet customer requirements.*

Actions:
- Develop standards for customer service that exceed customer expectations.
- Be clear about your objectives.
- Be clear about what you are measuring.
- Make sure that your customer is equally clear about your scope.
- Develop a reputation for exceeding expectations.

Skill: *Engage directly with the customer.*

Actions:
- Perform in a role where you are directly involved with developing a product for a customer.
- Meet face-to-face with customers to define significant problems and opportunities; clarify evolving customer requirements; participate in a team effort to deliver products/services to the customer; develop and track measurements concerning the impact that new products/services have in order to make sure they add value; and quantify the value added in customer terms.

Skill: *Examine everything you do to determine if it contributes to meeting customer needs.*

Action:
- Examine everything you do against these criteria: "Does this contribute to meeting customer needs?" or "What value does this add to the customer?"

Skill: *Find out the reasons a customer has stopped using your products or services.*

Actions:
- Interview the customers who have stopped using your products or services.
- Find out their reasons for leaving. This may help you identify the gaps between their requirements and what you are able to provide.
- If you find yourself saying "Yes, but . . ." more than two times, then you are probably not listening or (more importantly) not acknowledging your customer's opinion. You cannot give your perspective until you accurately paraphrase their perspective back to them.

(continued)

Leadership Competency 105:
Focusing on the Customer (continued)

Skill: *Formulate customer-specific pre- and post-call plans into daily plans.*

Action:
- Always begin your call by asking your customer an open-ended question. It will give them an opportunity to say what's weighing on their mind. It also gives you an opportunity to gauge your customer for content (the situation) and affect (the intensity of their feeling).

Skill: *Help customers select the appropriate product.*

Actions:
- Help customers understand which of the company's products are most appropriate for their needs.
- Match your customer's "pain point" with your solution, and have them rate the degree of improvement that they would experience as a result of your product/service.
- Select the product, rate the level of improvement, try to measure it, and summarize the solution.

Skill: *List the requirements you believe your customers have.*

Actions:
- Ask your customers what their requirements are.
- Note the differences.
- Ask each customer to clarify the difference for you.

Skill: *Make it easy for customers to register their complaints with you.*

Actions:
- Acknowledge both their content (the actual description of their complaint) and their affect (the feeling and level of intensity of that feeling).
- After a complaint has been resolved, call the customer to check up on his or her satisfaction level.

Skill: *Map your customer's key processes with a customer team.*

Actions:
- Make a flowchart of your process and have your customer do the same.
- Highlight all of the touchpoints between the two teams.
- Clearly state the expected "handoffs" between your team and theirs.
- Describe the handoffs in observable, measurable terms.

Skill: *Meet with front-line people to assess customer service improvements.*

Actions:
- Meet with your front-line people to solicit their ideas for improving customer service, and discuss how you can support their efforts with customers.
- Have the employees give examples of how they have met expectations and also of when they failed to meet an expectation.
- Describe what steps might prevent the failures from happening again.

(continued)

Leadership Competency 105:
Focusing on the Customer *(continued)*

Skill: *Participate in problem-solving meetings with customers.*

Actions:
- Do not try to run the meeting or steer the meeting your way. Simply listen and observe their attempts at solving the problem.
- You will inevitably be asked for your perspective. Use this opportunity to (1) summarize all of the stated perspectives, (2) give your perspective of the problem, (3) clarify what you believe is the reason for the problem, (4) state the needed direction for fixing the problem, and (5) identify how your organization can help.

Skill: *Perform a customer-needs analysis.*

Actions:
- Perform a customer-needs analysis. List the needs by category (e.g., resource, information, expertise).
- Weigh each need by impact and importance (use a 1-to-5 scale).
- Map your products/service value for each need.
- Choose the highest items to further explore the problem, reason, direction, and your organization's value-added proposition.
- Identify the next steps.

Skill: *Plan and use specific targeted selling messages in sales calls.*

Actions:
- Before the call, review the main messages in the sales materials.
- During the call, note your customer's reactions and perspective.
- End the call by committing to send them additional material that addresses their needs or concerns.
- After the call, send the materials and make a follow-up call.

Skill: *Provide special customer-service training to all employees.*

Action:
- Include tips on how to handle difficult requests and objections, and how to carry out service-related company policies and work processes.

Skill: *Reinforce the company's expectations regarding customer commitment.*

Action:
- In face-to-face interactions, reinforce the company's commitment to its customers as often as possible. Include these messages in the newsletter.

Skill: *Spend time working in your customer's area.*

Actions:
- Find an opportunity to speak informally with your customer's employees.
- Ask them for the best and worst perceptions of your company.
- Acknowledge their perspective before giving yours.
- Suggest ways for improving the situation on both ends.
- Do not make commitments that you cannot meet.

(continued)

Leadership Competency 105:
Focusing on the Customer (*concluded*)

Skill: *Take time every day to ask customers "How are we doing?"*

Actions:
- Actively listen to what they say.
- Communicate these findings to the appropriate people in your organization.

Skill: *Treat your internal customers with care and respect.*

Actions:
- Treat your internal customers with care and respect, just as you would treat your external customers.
- Gain a reputation for being reliable and dependable.
- Make your organization indispensable.
- Exceed expectations.
- Keep records of these achievements.

Skill: *Use marketing materials and messages on calls.*

Actions:
- Before the call, review the main messages in the sales materials.
- During the call, note your customer's reactions and perspective.
- End the call by committing to send them additional material that addresses their needs and concerns.
- After the call, send the materials and make a follow-up call.

Skill: *Add value to the customer.*

Action:
- Develop long-term, trusting relationships with customers or internal clients by establishing and maintaining credible ongoing relationships with key influencers and decision-makers in the customer's organization; developing and demonstrating "boardroom presence" (major presentations and/or one-on-one meetings); consulting with key customer leaders to develop market/product/service positioning; and identifying actions that will significantly impact the customer's business operations and assisting in their implementation.

Skill: *When hiring, look for the qualities necessary for good customer service.*

Actions:
- When hiring, look for necessary customer-service qualities, such as commitment to excellence, maturity, positive outlook, tolerance, and flexibility.
- Rate the candidate according to how well they attend, listen, respond, and initiate with value-added ideas.

Leadership Competency 106:
Selling

Skill: *Qualify leads.*

Actions:
- Identify the criteria that will help you determine if a lead is worth pursuing. For example, does this lead have a budget? Does he or she have decision-making authority? Does this person have a perceived need for my product, service, or solution?
- Investigate leads on the criteria before you make an investment in time and money.

Skill: *Build initial rapport with the customer.*

Actions:
- Establish a personal connection with the customer.
- Ask first about their situation and their needs before you give your presentation.
- Engage in a few minutes of social pleasantries before getting to the pitch.

Skill: *Understand customer needs.*

Actions:
- Inquire about the problems the customer is trying to solve and what he or she has already done to solve the problem.
- Ask about the business implications of not solving the problem or responding well enough to a business opportunity.
- Clarify with the customer what she or he is hoping your solution will do or provide.

Skill: *Manage time.*

Actions:
- Set priorities and review them regularly.
- Organize your day by devoting a specific period of time to phone calls and e-mails.
- When you are on the road, make as many customer calls as you can in a given location.
- Ask yourself, "Am I spending my time on what's most important and most urgent?"

Skill: *Establish a competitive strategy.*

Actions:
- Determine how your value proposition differentiates you from the competition.
- Create a compelling event that demonstrates your competitive advantage.
- Gain customer commitment for your proposal by showing how the customer will benefit from purchasing and using your product, service, or solution.

(continued)

Leadership Competency 106:
Selling *(concluded)*

Skill: *Develop excellent presentation skills.*

Actions:
- Take a course in presentation skills.
- Learn how to develop PowerPoint® presentations and use an LCD projector.
- Make your presentations concise but powerful.
- Practice delivering your presentation in front of a trusted colleague and ask him or her to give you feedback on content and style.

Skill: *Close the sale.*

Actions:
- Articulate clearly your value proposition to the customer.
- Customize the benefits to meet their needs. Identify any objections the customer has to your proposal, and develop ways to overcome the objections.
- Take a negotiating skills course that will help you get to "yes."

Skill: *Build customer relationships.*

Actions:
- Develop a personal relationship with your customer that is independent of where you are in the sales cycle.
- Ask yourself, "Am I considered a trusted advisor to this customer?"
- Develop credibility by being reliable and by adding value to conversations you are having with the customer, and by making sure your solution gets implemented to the satisfaction of the customer.

Leadership Competency 107:
Competing Effectively

Skill:	*Encourage cooperation, rather than competition.*
Actions:	• Encourage cooperation, rather than competition, between different work units. • Make sure groups set their goals in harmony with one another, and make sure that the goals are mutually supportive.

Skill:	*Think like your competitors.*
Actions:	• If you were to compete against yourself, what would you do? Ask yourself where you are most vulnerable. • Create strategies for addressing your company's vulnerabilities. • Anticipate how your competitors will respond to your strategic moves before you make any move in the marketplace.

Skill:	*Identify what your competitors are doing that is effective.*
Actions:	• What are the strengths of your competitors? Learn about your competitors as individuals. • Get to know their backgrounds and how they achieved competitive advantage in the past. Who are your competitors' customers? • Identify why these customers are not your customers yet, and whether or not your competitors are "better" in some way. • Study how your competition sells its products internationally.

Skill:	*Analyze impacts on the business.*
Action:	• To remain competitive, it is essential that you constantly scan the environment to understand changes that may affect your organization and its strategy. In order to stay up-to-date on the forces within and outside your industry that can impact your business, research the latest developments in your industry and related industry. Talk with people about changes, read industry reports and business publications, use consulting expertise, and use action-learning teams.

Skill:	*Know the strengths and weaknesses of your competitors.*
Actions:	• Keep an eye on all three groups of competitors: current competitors, future competitors in your industry, and potential competitors in different industries. • Be aware that the greatest threat is usually from unexpected competition. • Create a detailed profile of your company's top five to top ten competitors, and evaluate their competitive edge against your own.

(continued)

Leadership Competency 107:
Competing Effectively *(continued)*

Skill: *Convey a thorough understanding of your area's strengths, weaknesses, opportunities, and threats.*

Actions:
- To maintain a competitive edge, regularly identify and assess the elements of key business processes, their supporting processes and systems, your people, and your customers.
- Review critiques of your organization and its strategy in the media, in business publications, and within the investor community.
- Clearly identify the value you provide to your customers.
- Ask yourself why they should use you, and how your strategies will continue to add value for them.

Skill: *Identify your team's critical success factors.*

Actions:
- Chart the business processes for which your team is responsible, and highlight the pivotal parts of the process using language that describes the ideal contributions he/she makes to the goals of the team.
- Compile your team's list into a master list on a scale of 1–5 (5 = *absolutely necessary* and 1 = *not important*). Weigh the importance of each responsibility relative to the strategic goals and needs of important stakeholders. Review this list from others' perspectives. Would other important stakeholders agree?
- Make any changes necessary, based on this review.

Skill: *Pursue initiatives to capitalize on strengths and market opportunities.*

Actions:
- When strategic opportunity arises, not only must you recognize it as such, but you must do something about it quickly.
- Ask yourself a series of critical questions in order to identify key opportunities, such as these:
  — What do we anticipate will be the key drivers of our customers' decisions in the future?
  — How do our strengths and weaknesses compare with our competitors?
  — What competitive threats must we address?
- Have your team evaluate this information and determine where opportunities or threats lie.
- Based on this analysis, determine what initiatives and actions will have the most impact, and what steps you should take to capitalize on strengths and market opportunities.

Leadership Competency 107:
Competing Effectively *(concluded)*

Skill: *Stay focused on what is most important.*

Actions:
- Keep your list of key success factors on hand at all times. Use it to help you make decisions from a more strategic point of view, and use it to make sure your team is always keeping its focus on the "20 percent that makes 80 percent of the difference."
- Whenever you consider or implement something new, identify the key success factors for the new endeavor, and determine how they will be achieved. This will help you to manage the right things.

Skill: *Develop a wide-angle perspective of the company as a whole.*

Actions:
- Learn the business from the perspective of people in other functional areas. How do they see the business? How is their perspective the same or different from yours? Who are their customers? What are their challenges, goals, and strategies? How is their knowledge, experience, and perspective different than yours?
- Form cross-disciplinary teams to work on complex or recurring problems within the company and to pursue important business opportunities and initiatives.

Skill: *Recruit the best people.*

Actions:
- Identify key individuals or groups you will need to implement your business strategy, maintain your competitive edge, or and improve market share.
- Focus on attracting, deploying, developing, and retaining these people.
- In order to provide a fresh look at your organization, form an action-learning team composed of potential leaders in the organization to conduct an analysis of areas of concern.

Conclusion

What is leadership? Simply stated, leadership is the art of getting others to want to do what you believe needs to be done. Leaders gain the confidence of others through their insights, their interpersonal influence, and their competence. Leadership is not about having the power and influence to command and control the performance of those who are subordinate to you. Leadership responses exist at all levels in a company. Leadership is a choice any person can make in the moment.

What do leaders do? Leaders identify opportunities, build capabilities, and drive for results. There is no real mystery here. Although traditional images of leadership such as charisma may help, it is certainly not the prime variable in determining the influence that leaders have on the attitude, beliefs, and performance of others. Leadership is more about competencies than charisma. Leadership is more about talent than title. Leadership is more about behavior than bravado.

If others rely on leaders, what do leaders rely on? Effective leaders need input, processing, and feedback. They need to listen to others: their employees, their peers, their customers, their critics, their shareholders. Leaders need to be open to information of all types—positive, negative, and neutral. Leaders need processing capabilities to discriminate good ideas from bad ideas. They need to generate new responses to changing conditions, and to create new environments for change. Finally, leaders need to be open to feedback. They need to invite opinions on the behaviors they need to start, stop, and continue in order to be successful.

The Merck Leadership Center identifies 14 characteristics of effective leadership:

1. Actions reflect a high degree of integrity and ethics
2. Builds effective working relationships
3. Capitalizes on opportunities to contribute
4. Communicates a vision
5. Communicates openly and effectively
6. Continuously learns
7. Focuses on the customer
8. Integrates ideas and collaborates with others

9. Recognizes and rewards performance
10. Sets clear objectives
11. Thinks and acts strategically
12. Trains and develops employees
13. Treats employees with dignity and respect
14. Uses feedback effectively

We believe this set of characteristics is a good one. Clearly, leaders who were able to live by all those characteristics would attract followers and would perform their role well. We're not sure, however, if any list makes a real difference. In this book, we have tried to do two things:

1. Keep the list short, i.e., the three meta-competencies of leadership.

2. Provide a resource for leaders to find actionable suggestions that might be helpful in a given situation.

The real issue of leadership is still the challenge of processing new information and generating new responses to changing conditions. This book provides a solid construct for processing information (identify, build, and drive) and a wealth of ideas for generating new responses (107 competencies). We hope you have found the book useful.